EAT at JOE'S

The Joe's Stone Crab
Restaurant Cookbook

BY JO ANN BASS AND RICHARD SAX

PHOTOGRAPHS BY BUD LEE

CLARKSON POTTER / PUBLISHERS
NEW YORK

PREVIOUS PAGE: Joe's bright neon sign is a landmark at the southern end of Miami Beach. LEFT: Seabreeze, Rabbi, and Irwin "Say" Sawitz. OPPOSITE: The entrance to the restaurant.

Published by Clarkson N. Potter, Inc., 201 East 50th Street, New York, New York 10022. Member of the Crown Publishing Group.

Random House, Inc. New York, Toronto, London, Sydney, Auckland.

CLARKSON N. POTTER, POTTER, and colophon are trademarks of Clarkson N. Potter, Inc.

Manufactured in the United States of America

Design by Renato Stanisic

Library of Congress Cataloging-in-Publication Data

Bass, Jo Ann
Eat at Joe's / by Jo Ann Bass and Richard Sax; photographs by Bud Lee.
Includes bibliographical references and index.
1. Cookery (Seafood) 2. Cookery, American. 3. Joe's Stone Crab Restaurant.
I. Sax, Richard. II. Title.
TX747.B342 1994
641.6'92—dc20 93–19322 CIP

ISBN 0-517-59563-X

10 9 8 7 6 5 4 3 2 1

First Edition

THIS BOOK IS DEDICATED—

*To my grandparents, Joe and Jennie, and my
parents, Jesse and Grace—without whom
there would have been no Joe's to write a history of
—To all the loyal and dedicated
employees (the Joe's family), without
whom there would be no present at Joe's
—To my children, Jodi and Steve, into whose hands
we trust the future of Joe's
—To Bob, my favorite doctor, whose
prescription of laughter keeps me going.
To all of you, I give my love.*
Jo Ann Bass

Acknowledgments

This book could not have been written without the generosity of the Joe's family—the owners, employees, line cooks, and waiters—all of whom contributed a great deal.

Special thanks to Bob; Stephen, Jodi, and Say; Grace and Jesse; Rose and Dick; Calvin; Bob, Alan, Lisa, and Lori; and all the cooks.

Thanks also to Richard Brown, Miami Beach City Clerk, and Dorothy Merante in his office; Dr. Paul George; Tim Brigham, Martha Limner of the Miami Visitors and Convention Bureau; Alys Daly; Nancy Rose; Susan Magrino; Maida Heatter; and Sharon Bossert.

Luli Gray helped test recipes, as did Sandra Rose Gluck, James Lartin, and Mary Rehak. Barbara Prisco tirelessly transcribed tapes. And Roy Finamore was as insightful an editor as one could wish for—he made this book a joy to work on.

Credits

The recipe for Barbecued Alaska Salmon, p. 38, is adapted from *The Great American Seafood Cookbook* by Susan Herrmann Loomis, © 1988. Reprinted with permission of Workman Publishing Company.

The recipe for Key Lime Cake, p. 120, is adapted from *Keys Cuisine—Flavors of the Florida Keys* by Linda Gassenheimer, © 1991 (Atlantic Monthly Press). Reprinted by permission of the author.

The Damon Runyon excerpt on pages 23–25 is used by permission of Damon Runyon and King Features.

Photograph credits—Lenny Cohen: page 76; Ray Fisher: jacket photo of Jesse Weiss, pages 67 (top and bottom) and 69; Chris Hansen: page 75 (bottom); Eli Silverberg: pages 65 (inset) and 66.

Preface

I had eaten at Joe's Stone Crab in Miami Beach a number of times over the years and had always enjoyed it, both for its great stone crabs with mustard sauce and for its role as a Miami institution. But I did not know the length, breadth, and depth of the family story.

Then, when Joan De Mayo had the idea for this book and Roy Finamore contacted me about working on it with Jo Ann Bass, I learned that Joe's has been a family operation for eighty years, going steadily since 1913 and now in its fourth generation. I also learned that it was Joe Weiss who discovered that this crustacean, *Menippe mercenaria*, is edible.

There's another dimension, though. People who work in restaurants, like people who work in theatre and in many other businesses, often say, "Our business is like a family." That just happens, because you wind up spending so much time working together; in many cases, you're with them more than you're with your blood relations. But from the moment I arrived at Joe's and began to spend time with the staff, on a series of visits, I understood that this really *is* a family—both in the literal sense of the Weiss family and in the extended family of staff, many of whom have been with Joe's for twenty, thirty, and even forty years. I have never been so welcomed into any family, anywhere.

This is a remarkable story, and I am delighted to have been given this chance to tell it.

—Richard Sax
New York City, Spring 1993

Contents

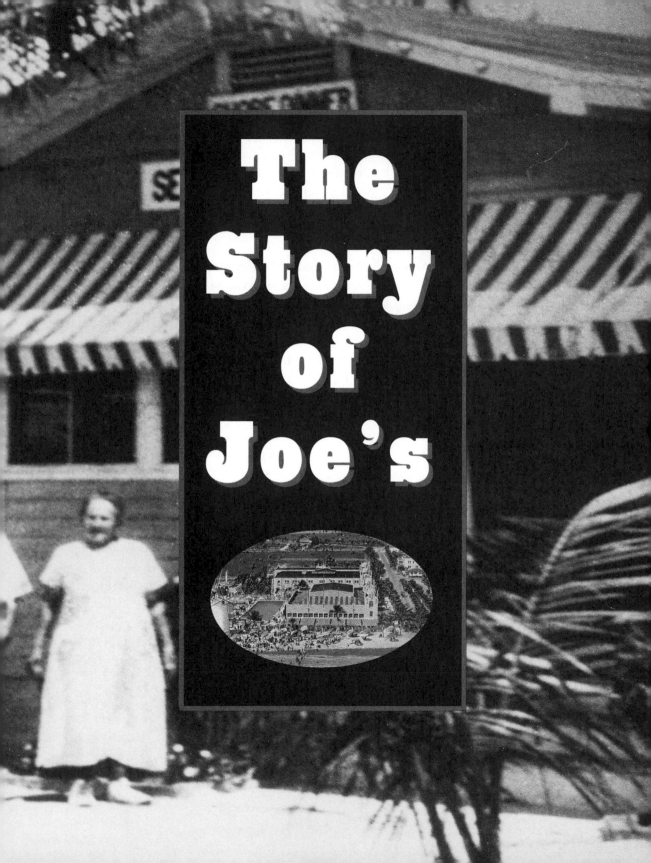

The Story of Joe's

It's

rare that a restaurant is still around—thriving—after eighty years. Even rarer is when it stays in the same family for all that time. According to one Florida historian, Joe's is "Miami Beach's only continuous authentic link with the old days." The story of Joe's Stone Crab is the story of four generations of the Weiss family, with a fifth not far behind. And some story it is.

The Beginnings—a Lunch Stand at Smith's Casino

Joseph Weiss—the "Joe" of Joe's Stone Crab—came to Miami in 1913, when his doctors told him that the only help for his asthma would be a change of climate. Joe and his wife, Jennie, both Hungarian-born, were living in New York, where their son Jesse was born in 1907. Joe was a waiter, and Jennie cooked in small restaurants.

Some seventy years later, Jesse recalled the move:

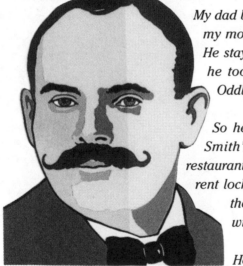

My dad borrowed fifty dollars on his life insurance policy, left my mother and me in New York, and came to Florida. . . . He stayed in Miami one night, and he couldn't breathe. So he took the ferry boat that used to go to Miami Beach. Oddly enough, he could breathe over here.

So he stayed here and started running a lunch stand at Smith's bathing casino. That was the beginning of the restaurant that was the seed for Joe's. You'd come over and rent lockers to change your clothes to use the ocean or use the pool! The gals used to have the long bathing suits with the stockings...that was 1913.

He sent for my mother and myself—she had this brat on her hands. We came down by train; I was six years old when we arrived. Collins Avenue was not really a street—it was sort of a trail with ruts in it.

In 1918, Joe and Jennie bought a bungalow near the casino, on Biscayne Street. They moved into the back, set up seven or eight tables on the front porch, cooked in the kitchen, and called it Joe's Restaurant. Jennie waited on tables, Joe cooked, and every

EAT AT JOE'S

thing started to grow from there. When it got crowded, they'd spill over into the dining room. They served snapper, pompano, mackerel, and some meat dishes.

"We used to open for breakfast, lunch, and dinner in those days," Jesse remembered, "because we were the only restaurant on the beach. For about eight years there was no competition. And my father made a hell of a fish sandwich."

At the age of twelve, after he'd had a paper route delivering the *Miami Herald* by bicycle, Jesse began to wait tables for his parents. "We had to have smudge pots at the doors—the mosquitoes would eat you alive. Ceiling fans kept us cool."

These were still the days before the development of Miami Beach; the township had been incorporated only in 1915. "I would say maybe thirty-five people were living on the Beach year round in those days," Jesse remembered. (The permanent population in 1920, according to city records, was 644.) "They had mosquitoes and shells, nothing else. There were only three other boys on the beach, and no schools, so we used to take the ferry to Miami."

PREVIOUS PAGES: Lincoln Road circa 1930. Joseph and Jennie Weiss outside the original Joe's Restaurant; INSET: Smith's bathing casino, Miami Beach. Opposite: Joseph Weiss. ABOVE: Washington Avenue, circa 1930.

In 1913, the Collins Bridge was built across Biscayne Bay, linking Miami Beach with Miami. Once the County Causeway was built in 1920 (to be rechristened MacArthur Causeway in 1942), Miami Beach began its ascent as "America's Winter Playground."

Jesse Weiss remembered it well:

The town started booming. Oh man, it was a vibrant, living time. It was like a cocoon that broke open. Hurray for hell, who's scared of fire, you know?

A *particularly memorable night at Joe's Stone Crab in Miami Beach was the night of the first Liston-Clay fight, in 1964. I will never again see a crowd like that in a restaurant, from Frank Sinatra to J. Edgar Hoover to Howard Cosell. . . . That was the fight in which Liston was a fifteen-to-one favorite and after which Clay said he was now going to be called Muhammad Ali.*

—*Larry King,* Tell It to the King

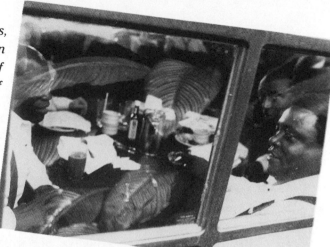

The season was very short—ten weeks, twelve at the most. January 15, when Hialeah opened, was really the peak of the season. It was the grand old lady of racing. The Vanderbilts and those people...stayed up in Palm Beach, and would come down on the train that ran from Palm Beach to Hialeah racetrack. Some of them came over to the Beach. We used to get them all in that small cottage.

The Flamingo was the first big hotel, built by Carl Fisher [who built the Indianapolis Speedway] so his people could come in from the Midwest. Miami Beach used to have the Fords, the Firestones, Boss Kettering of General Motors, Alfred P. Sloane [the latter two subsidized Sloane-Kettering Hospital in New York]...you name it, the entire General Motors empire, they

OPPOSITE: The trolley line along South Alton Road in the late 1930s. ABOVE: Inside Joe's, Eddie Rolle, Moses Battle, and Nat Allen.

were here in the wintertime. (This is not for quote...most of the guys had a sweetheart out here when they wanted to get away from their old lady. But that's another story.)

Miami also attracted another crowd early on: the movie industry, still in its infancy.

About 1921, motion picture studios used to come down here and shoot pictures on the Beach. They used to tie up with foremasted schooners at the foot of Biscayne Street, and they'd have all the lights on and they'd have the gorilla jumping from one mast to the other.... Richard Barthelmess was usually the hero in his loin cloth. There were other famous actors of the day: Wallace Reed, the Gish sisters...they looked like porcelain; they were always with D. W. Griffith. I was in one picture with Ramon Novarro; I skipped school and ran around in a loin cloth. They paid five bucks a day.

They ate their meals with us three times a day. Why they didn't get bored with it, I'll never know. They probably were but were too nice to say anything.

The "Discovery" of Stone Crabs

By this time, Joe's was off and running. "We got the 'in' crowd, the society crowd," Jesse remembered. "At that time, we could seat maybe forty or fifty." But stone crabs were yet to come. In fact, no one then knew that this local crustacean was even edible.

Fried Oysters

SERVES 2

4 cups vegetable oil, or as needed
  for deep-frying
2/3 cup all-purpose flour
2 eggs
2 tablespoons cold water
1/2 teaspoon salt

1 cup seasoned dry bread crumbs
1 dozen shucked oysters
Cocktail sauce or tartar sauce,
  for serving
Lime or lemon wedges,
  for garnish

Heat the oil in a deep skillet or casserole to a temperature of 365 to 375°F. Set up breading: Place the flour in a pie plate or shallow bowl. Beat the egg with the water and salt in a shallow bowl; place this next to the flour. Alongside, nearest the stove, place the bread crumbs in a third pie plate or shallow bowl.

When the oil reaches 375°F, a pinch of flour will sizzle energetically as soon as it hits the oil; a cube of bread will turn golden in 25 to 30 seconds. Adjust the heat to maintain a steady temperature. Working fairly quickly, dip 6 of the oysters in the flour. Toss them to coat and shake off excess flour, either with your fingers or with a mesh skimmer. Dip the oysters in the egg mixture; then roll them in bread crumbs to coat lightly, gently shaking off excess.

Fry the oysters until golden brown, about 2 minutes. Drain well and keep them warm while you bread and fry the remaining oysters. Serve hot with cocktail sauce or tartar sauce. Garnish with lime or lemon wedges.

When Craig Claiborne came down to judge a March of Dimes cooking gala, he and cookbook author Maida Heatter wanted to come in for stone crabs. "I was deflated when they told me it was closed for lunch on Saturday. Stone crabs are one of the few things I feel gluttonous about. It's their texture, flavor and succulence." So Joe's opened the restaurant. As food writer Geoffrey Tomb put it in the Miami Herald, on March 3, 1982, "When you are Craig Claiborne you can get closed restaurants to open. . . . He and his old friend Maida Heatter . . . sat in lonely splendor in the empty restaurant eating stone crabs and drinking Pouilly-Fuissé."

EAT AT JOE'S

Joe's Mustard Sauce

At Joe's, the stone crabs are served cold, already cracked. They come with small metal cups of mustard sauce or melted butter—or both. This is the mustard sauce for which Joe's is famous.

MAKES ABOUT 1 CUP

1 tablespoon plus ½ teaspoon
 Colman's dry mustard, or more
 to taste
1 cup mayonnaise
2 teaspoons Worcestershire sauce

1 teaspoon A-1 sauce
2 tablespoons each heavy cream
 and milk
Salt

Place the mustard in a mixing bowl or the bowl of an electric mixer. Add the mayonnaise and beat for 1 minute.

Add the Worcestershire, A-1, cream, and a pinch of salt and beat until the mixture is well blended and creamy. If you'd like a little more mustardy bite, whisk in about ½ teaspoon more dry mustard until well blended. Chill the sauce, covered, until serving.

RIGHT: Miami personality Michael Scott, sporting a Joe's bib, stops mid-dip to pose for the camera.

In 1921, James Allison, Fisher's partner in the Speedway, built an aquarium at the foot of the bay and Fifth Street. "He got all hopped up on having marine research done," Jesse said. "I used to go up in the lab and watch them work."

Allison invited a Harvard ichthyologist down to do research.

One of them came down one day and said to my dad, "Have you ever used these stone crabs, these crabs from the water?" We were serving crawfish, all kinds of fish—but not stone crabs.

"Nobody will eat them," Dad said. That was at breakfast. That day when the ichthyologist came down for lunch, he brought a burlap sack, full of live stone crabs. He and my dad went around and around about how to cook them. Do you broil them, or what do you do with them?

My dad threw the stone crabs in boiling water and that was the beginning of it. The bay was full of them! When we started serving them cracked with hash brown potatoes, cole slaw, and mayonnaise, they were an instant success. We charged seventy-five cents for four or five crabs, twenty-five cents for potatoes and twenty-five cents an order for cole slaw. And this is the way we have been serving them since. We hit the jackpot with that one!

"The Gentry Eats Crabs"

By the mid-1920s, and through the 1930s, Miami Beach was thriving, with pink and white Art Deco hotels lining the beach. A streetcar went across the causeway from Miami. Jesse remembered:

One of the big things was to promenade on Lincoln Road, past the great shops. You'd see these men getting out of their chauffeur-driven cars and promenading in white flannel

18

pants, white shoes, a double-breasted blazer, a tie, starched collar, straw hat, a cane. At that time, particularly during the gambling era, we had entertainment that you wouldn't believe. Sophie Tucker, Al Jolson, George Jessel—you name it, they were here. Hildegarde was quite a favorite. Tommy Dorsey and his orchestra.

The crowd included the captains of the automotive industry, as well as such notables as John Oliver LaGorce, publisher of *National Geographic*. And everyone wanted to taste the Miami Beach sensation, stone crabs at Joe's. "These people all wound up in here," Jesse said.

As in the early days, Joe did the cooking, Jennie ran the dining room. "She was a tough old broad," Jesse remembered:

She reminded me of some of those old Zane Grey books, where the madam is tough as hell but all heart. If she didn't like you she wouldn't let you in. Let's say a man was married and coming in with his wife. Then, another time, he'd try to come in with his girlfriend—out! She's just as soon say, don't bring your tramp friends in here. Who's going to fight with an old lady? So that was that.

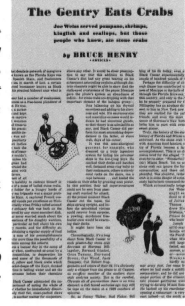

Other clients were captains of a different sort of industry. But Jennie Weiss had her own criteria for who belonged at Joe's:

Al Capone came in, and he used the name Al Brown. Every day at 5 o'clock (because no one dined 'til about 5:30, 6:00 P.M.), he'd pull up with his entourage and sit down and have dinner and go.

One night Jennie walked up to Mr. Capone. She said, "Mr. Brown, I must tell you something. If I don't like somebody, I don't allow them to come in here, but you've always been a gentleman, and anytime you want to come into this restaurant, you can." She never realized who he really was but she had heard somebody mention, that's so and so. It touched him. Every Mother's Day, up pulled a truck with flowers, a horseshoe reading, "Good Luck Mother Joe's."

In 1939, *Esquire* published an article about Joe's called "The Gentry Eats Crabs." The word was spreading.

Changing Times

Well into the 1930s, Miami Beach was still very restricted. "Anti-Semitic, antiblack," Jesse remembered. "The Klan was very big around here; between 1920 and 1928, the Klan was in its glory. We were the first Jewish family on the Beach."

In the twenties and for decades after, blacks were only allowed here to work and they had to have a permit. And they had to be off the Beach after dark. I used to drive our employees across the causeway at night, 10 o'clock, 10:30 . . . I'd take them home and never had any problems. Never!

Jesse went off to law school in Tennessee. But first he married his sweetheart, Frances Levitt, in 1926, when they were both nineteen. "Her father was not for it," Jesse explained, "because he was shooting at higher game. He was a very wealthy man from Canada. But she decided that she would prefer to have me. We had known each other for several years, and it was love at first sight.

"Law was very boring. I really was interested in the restaurant business, which I came back to. My dad and I got along great. We were very, very happy, and we had a wonderful time, a good life. We were married about four years before Frances had our daughter Jo Ann. Jo Ann is very much like her mother, a very soft-spoken person."

By 1930, Joe's had outgrown its space. Jesse's father-in-law built the building that is still the main body of Joe's today, with a courtyard fountain between the main dining room and the original porch. Just across Biscayne Street was the Plaza Theatre, which later became Minsky's Burlesque. Dinners were still served on the old porch in summer, but the new, larger dining room was necessary for the busy winter season. Upstairs was a two-family apartment. "My grandparents lived at one end," Jo Ann remembers clearly, "and my parents at the other; they had a common living room and kitchen. And that's where I grew up." Today, this space houses the restaurant's offices.

"Then Frances's stomach started," Jesse said. "The first colostomy ever performed in the United States was performed on her at Johns Hopkins, in Baltimore. Eighteen months later she needed another operation. She passed away, she died in surgery.

There's one key to our success—and that's our employees. You can't do it without the people. That's the bottom line. It's them. The real success belongs to our employees. That's who makes it happen.

—Irwin "Say" Sawitz

EAT AT JOE'S

**Jo Ann Bass
growing up at Joe's.**

"I was twenty-five when she died. Frances was not quite twenty-six. Jo Ann was six-teen months old when she lost her mother. After that," Jesse said, "I really kind of went haywire because after she passed away, I got married many times, until I settled down with Grace." Jo Ann: "My dad never spoke much about my natural mother. He'd tear up and that would be the end of it."

Jo Ann Weiss was raised by her grandmother. "My mother was tough on Jo Ann," Jesse remembered later. "I think that's why Jo Ann's got so much compassion—because she realizes what a tough old broad can be like."

Then, in 1930, Joe died, and Jesse started running the restaurant with his mother. Eight years later, Jennie died, but by that time, Jesse was running the restaurant on his own. And that's when his unique personality took over. Jo Ann remembered:

I don't know how helpful my dad was. He didn't know a lot about the kitchen. But he was wonderful out front with the customers.

He was typical of the restaurant men of his era—they had their volatile sides, but they also had this wonderful front. My father was a terrific storyteller. He had a great sense of humor and was very colorful—he just had an extraordinary personality. Dad was able to make friends with everybody that came into the restaurant. J. Edgar Hoover, Burt Lancaster—it was nothing for my dad to just walk over to a table, sit down, make himself at home, and become a buddy.

My father was a cross between a Mike Romanoff and a Toots Shor. He didn't have Mike Romanoff's gentility, but he wasn't quite as diamond-in-the-rough as Toots Shor.

THE STORY OF JOE'S

J. Edgar Hoover, here with his boxer, was a longtime friend of Jesse's.

Jesse had his wild side, too. He'd take the day's cash receipts, get dressed, and head out to the racetrack. And he had a well-known eye for the ladies. "I was actually married seven times," he recalled. "I used to use Jo Ann as bait when I went to the beach. I'd take this cute little girl wih her little Scottie dog, and some cute gal would walk up and talk to her, and I'd walk over, like 'This is a sample of my work.' I've had dates that were longer than some of my marriages."

Anyone well known who came to Miami Beach, from anywhere in the world, would stop in at Joe's. A list of Jesse's acquaintances, several of whom became lifelong close friends, forms a veritable Who's Who of the twentieth century. Will Rogers. ("Will

Rogers was Will Rogers," Jesse remembered. "As homespun as anybody could be—I liked him a lot.") Amelia Earhart. ("She was down to earth. You knew where you stood with her. If you'll pardon the expression, there was no bullshit to her.") The Duke and Duchess of Windsor. Gloria Swanson, America's closest thing to royalty. (Jesse: "I thought she was this little doll. She used to come in here with Joseph Kennedy, who was the great love, but I didn't know it then! Hell, I was worried about my own sex life.") J. Edgar Hoover. ("I was closer to J. Edgar Hoover than I was to anyone else. I used to call him Gatling Gun Joe.") Walter Winchell. ("People would say, 'How can you be friendly with that son of a bitch?' And I'd say, 'Because he's my son of a bitch.' ") And Damon Runyon, who helped fan the flames of the Joe's Stone Crab legend.

Damon Runyon on Stone Crabs, from "The Brighter Side"

One of the more regrettable circumstances attendant upon the tourist invasion of Dade County, Florida, of recent winters, was the discovery by visitors of the stone crab.

The home folks down in Dade County, Florida, have long esteemed the stone crab the greatest of native delicacies and can remember when they were so numerous that a man could dip a foot anywhere in Biscayne Bay and come up with a stone crab hanging on each toe. Or lacking the energy to dunk a pedal he could buy more stone crabs for a few bits more than a horse could lug.

Since the Winter visitors got on to the stone crab, however, the crustaceans have become scarce and costly. They now sell by the karat. They are so expensive that the home folks are inclined to leave them off their menus. The visitors eat more of the stone crab nowadays and this is all the more deplorable when you reflect that stone crabs are really too good for visitors. A certificate of at least four years residence in Dade County should be required of every person desiring stone crabs.

The stone crab is an ornery looking critter that hangs out around the Florida Keys and nowhere else in the world. It is a sucker for a trap baited with fish. It bears some resem-

---

IKE DINES ON STONE CRABS FLOWN TO HIM FROM MIAMI

President Eisenhower dined on Florida stone crabs from Jesse Weiss's Joe's Stone Crabs restaurant Tuesday. It was the idea of his Secretary of Defense [Charles E. Wilson], who was at Joe's last weekend, and expressed a desire to share the culinary wealth with his boss. So Jesse prepared, packed and air-expressed the under-water delicacy.

— *George Bourke*, Miami Herald, *November 30, 1955*

---

blance to the California crab, but is cooked and served differently and the taste is also different. Occasionally a Californian from up around San Francisco drifts into Dade County, Florida, and goes against stone crabs and right away he wants to go out in the kitchen and start an argument with the chef on the basis that the California cracked crab tastes better.

This is where we would not care to take sides. We always bear in mind the experience of a New York fellow who stepped between a Californian and a New Yorker who were arguing the respective merits of the California cracked crab and the Florida stone crab. The poor soul incautiously ventured the statement that the northern crab tastes better than either and he got slugged from two directions.

The stone crab is much larger than the northern crab and has a shell harder than a landlord's heart. In places in Dade County where stone crabs are served, the shell is cracked with a large wooden mallet before being set before the customer. Only the huge claws of the stone crab contain the edible meat. The body is waste, but when the live crab is weighed the body is included in the total poundage and the buyer pays by the pound.

The stone crab is cooked by boiling. A lot of people have tried to think up better ways, but boiling is best. It is served cold with hot melted butter with a dash of lemon in it on the side. Probably the right place in which to eat stone crabs would be the bathtub. The fingers are used in toying with them. Some high-toned folks use those little dinky oyster forks, but the fingers are far speedier and more efficient.

In Dade County, prior to 1920, no one bothered much with stone crabs as an article of

EAT AT JOE'S

diet. Then the late Jim Allison, of Indianapolis, one of the builders of Miami Beach, who had an aquarium on the shores of Biscayne Bay loaded with aquatic fauna of various kinds, imported a Harvard professor to study and classify the local fish and one day this professor saw some boys with a bunch of stone crabs.

He wanted to know what they were going to do with them, and they said they were going to throw them away. The professor said that was bad judgement as crabs were good eating, and somebody tried them and found he was right as rain. Biscayne Bay was full of stone crabs at that time, but harbor blasting and dredging chased them away and the great crabbing grounds are now to the south of Dade County, along the Keys, a Key being just a small island.

There is a restaurant at the south of Miami Beach known as Joe's which specializes in stone crabs. Joe's, the oldest and most famous restaurant on the beach, is conducted by Joe Weiss, whose father established the place around 1919. Weiss has his own boats operating during the stone crab season which runs from October 15 to May 15 and this gives him a big edge over the other restaurant men on the crabs. He uses as high as a thousand pounds of crabs a day.

The stone crab of Dade County seems to be the morro crab of Cuba with a Spanish accent. They are both ugly enough to enjoy some kinship. It is the looks of the stone crab that has deterred many a Winter visitor to Dade County from eating it—many, but not enough to suit those of us who view the inroads of the visitors on the crab supply with genuine alarm.

New Beginnings

During World War II, Jesse was in the service for four years. He was married at the time to Mildred, wife number four. While stationed at Champaign-Urbana, Illinois, Jesse met Grace, who became wife number five once he divorced Mildred. (After an interim episode, Grace also became wife number seven, and she is still, after nearly fifty years, with Jesse today.)

After the war, they headed down to Miami. Grace remembered the trip:

(text continues on page 34)

Grace Weiss
in the 1940s.

She-Crab Soup

This is a traditional specialty from the Chesapeake Bay. This rich version, which can be made with the meat of stone crab claws or with lump crabmeat, is based on a recipe from Sharon Bossert, of Bossert Boatyard in Marathon, Florida, 45 miles north of Key West.

SERVES 4 TO 6

4 tablespoons unsalted butter
¼ cup chopped onion
1 small carrot, peeled and cut in small dice
1 small celery rib, trimmed and cut in small dice
¼ cup all-purpose flour
½ teaspoon paprika
2 hard-cooked eggs, shelled
1 quart milk
1½ teaspoons salt, or to taste

¼ teaspoon Tabasco sauce, or to taste
8 to 10 ounces lump crabmeat, or the meat of 12 stone crab claws, carefully picked over
⅓ cup medium-dry sherry (or to taste), plus more for serving
Pepper
3 tablespoons chopped fresh parsley
2 scallion greens, sliced thin (optional)

Heat the butter in a large, heavy saucepan over medium heat. Add the onion, carrot, and celery and cook, stirring, for 5 minutes. Sprinkle on the flour and paprika and cook, stirring, for 3 or 4 minutes longer. With a fine grater, carefully grate the hard-cooked eggs onto a plate; gently stir the eggs into the mixture in the pan.

Slowly add the milk, salt, and Tabasco, whisking. Heat the soup, whisking occasionally, until it comes nearly to a simmer. Add the crabmeat and sherry and cook just below a simmer for 5 minutes longer. (The soup can be prepared in advance to this point. Reheat gently if necessary.)

Stir in the pepper, parsley, and scallions, if using, and correct all seasonings. Serve hot, adding a dash of sherry to each serving.

Is that gorgeous? Is that a thing of beauty? The black, the orange, then the beautiful pale yellow. That's one pound in a single claw.

—*Dick McDaniel*

EAT AT JOE'S

Grilled Stuffed Tomatoes

Jo Ann developed this recipe, which has become a classic side dish with stone crabs.

SERVES 6

3 large ripe beefsteak tomatoes
1 cup Creamed Spinach (page 82)
1½ cups seasoned bread crumbs
6 tablespoons melted unsalted butter

Salt and pepper
1 cup grated American or
  Cheddar cheese

Preheat the broiler, with a rack 5 or 6 inches from the heat source. Cut each tomato into 4 slices, discarding the cores, and arrange the slices on a baking sheet.

In a mixing bowl, stir together the spinach, bread crumbs, melted butter, and salt and pepper; the mixture will be quite thick. With a tablespoon, mound some of the spinach mixture over each tomato slice, nearly covering it. Top generously with grated cheese, gently pressing it on.

Broil until the cheese is bubbly and beginning to turn lightly golden, about 5 minutes (timing can vary; watch carefully to prevent burning). With a spatula, transfer the tomatoes to a platter and serve hot.

LEFT: Guillermo Aguilera, ready to prep an onion. ABOVE: Jo Ann and Felix Rodriguez in the kitchen.

6

7

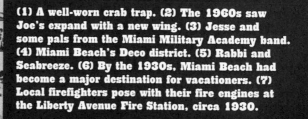

(1) A well-worn crab trap. (2) The 1960s saw Joe's expand with a new wing. (3) Jesse and some pals from the Miami Military Academy band. (4) Miami Beach's Deco district. (5) Rabbi and Seabreeze. (6) By the 1930s, Miami Beach had become a major destination for vacationers. (7) Local firefighters pose with their fire engines at the Liberty Avenue Fire Station, circa 1930.

Crab Cakes

SERVES 4 (MAKES 8 CRAB CAKES)

1 pound jumbo lump crabmeat,
 picked over
1/2 red bell pepper, chopped
1/4 cup chopped onion
4 scallions, trimmed and chopped
1/4 cup chopped fresh parsley
1 garlic clove, minced
1 egg, lightly beaten
2 tablespoons Dijon mustard
1 tablespoon fresh lemon juice

1/2 teaspoon Worcestershire
 sauce
Scant 1/4 teaspoon Tabasco sauce
3/4 cup fine dry bread crumbs
2 tablespoons unsalted butter,
 plus more if needed
2 tablespoons vegetable oil, plus
 more if needed
Lime or lemon wedges, for garnish

In a large mixing bowl, combine the crabmeat, red pepper, onion, scallions, parsley, and garlic. In a small bowl, stir together the egg, mustard, lemon juice, Worcestershire, and Tabasco. Gently fold this mixture into the crabmeat mixture; then add 1/4 cup of the bread crumbs, mixing with a light touch, just until combined.

Form 8 patties, using 1/2 cup of the crabmeat mixture for each. The patties should be made ovals about 1/2-inch thick and 3 1/2 inches long. Coat the patties with the remaining bread crumbs and place them on a wax paper–lined baking sheet. Refrigerate until set, at least 1 hour.

Heat the butter and oil in a large skillet, preferably nonstick, over medium heat. Add 4 of the crab cakes at a time. Cook until golden, about 5 minutes. Adjust the heat as you cook so that the fat maintains a steady, gentle sizzle. Gently flip the crab cakes with a spatula and cook until golden, about 5 minutes. Serve hot, garnished with lime or lemon wedges, with a small cup of salsa on the side, if you like.

SALSA FOR CRAB CAKES

MAKES ABOUT 2 CUPS

1 1/2 pounds firm ripe tomatoes, cored, seeded, and diced (about 3 cups)

1 cucumber, peeled, halved lengthwise, seeded, and cut in 1/4-inch dice

1/4 white onion, chopped

1/2 red or green bell pepper, cut in 1/4-inch dice

1 or 2 jalapeño peppers, seeded and minced (optional)

2 tablespoons chopped fresh cilantro, or to taste

1 small can (5.5 ounces) V-8 juice

2 teaspoons salt, or to taste

1 teaspoon black pepper, or to taste

1 1/2 tablespoons sugar

1 garlic clove, minced

Juice of 1 1/2 to 2 limes or lemons

1 tablespoon Worcestershire sauce

1 teaspoon Tabasco sauce, or to taste

Mix everything together in a mixing bowl. Chill for at least 2 hours before serving.

It was Joe's that the Duke and Duchess of Windsor selected for their only meal in a public place. Fellow gatherers included J. Edgar Hoover and Clyde Tolson, Lily Pons and André Kostelanetz.

—Columnist Louis Sobol, March 1941

Fried Shrimp

SERVES 2

4 cups vegetable oil, or as needed
  for deep-frying
²/₃ cup all-purpose flour
2 eggs
2 tablespoons cold water
¹/₂ teaspoon salt
1 cup cracker meal (or use
  crushed saltines or seasoned dry
  bread crumbs)

16 to 18 medium-large shrimp
  (12 to 16 ounces), peeled but
  with tails on, and deveined
Tartar sauce or cocktail sauce,
  for serving
Lime or lemon wedges,
  for garnish

Heat the oil in a deep skillet or casserole to a temperature of 375°F. Set up breading: Place the flour in a pie plate or shallow bowl. Beat the egg with the water and salt in a shallow bowl; place this next to the flour. Alongside, nearest the stove, place the bread crumbs in a third pie plate or shallow bowl.

When the oil reaches 375°F, a pinch of flour will sizzle energetically as soon as it hits the oil; a cube of bread will turn golden in 25 to 30 seconds. Adjust the heat to maintain a steady temperature. Working fairly quickly, dip 8 or 9 of the shrimp in the flour. Toss them to coat and shake off excess flour, either with your fingers or with a mesh skimmer. Dip the shrimp into the egg mixture; then roll them in cracker meal to coat lightly, gently pressing each shrimp flat.

Fry the shrimp until golden brown, 2 to 3 minutes. Drain well and keep them warm while you bread and fry the remaining shrimp. Serve hot with tartar sauce or cocktail sauce. Garnish with lime or lemon wedges.

A magnificent, glittering emporium seating three hundred diners bears Joe's name now, in Miami Beach. But next door stands the same shabby little house where he made his fame. Jesse runs it for those famous and infamous who know Menippe well.

As as one of Joe's waiters once said: "They comes, they goes; some eat steak, some eat fish . . . but the gentry eats crabs!"

—Bruce Henry, *"The Gentry Eats Crabs," Esquire, February 1939*

Shrimp de Jonghe

At Joe's, this dish is prepared with tiny shrimp, which Ronald Rose assembles to order. He also makes cold lobster platters and broiled stuffed Florida lobsters, wearing gloves to handle the spiny lobsters.

SERVES 2

50 to 60 tiny shrimp, or 12 ounces medium shrimp, peeled and deveined
2 tablespoons Garlic Butter (page 58)
Salt and pepper
1 ½ tablespoons fresh lime juice

5 sheets Waverley wafer crackers
2 tablespoons grated Parmesan cheese
1 tablespoon chopped fresh parsley
2 small parsley sprigs, for garnish
Lime or lemon wedges, for garnish

Preheat the oven to 400°F. Arrange the shrimp in a gratin dish or other shallow baking dish, mounding them slightly in the center. Drizzle the Garlic Butter over the shrimp. Sprinkle with salt and pepper, then with lime juice. Place the baking dish on a baking sheet.

Crush the Waverley wafers in a food processor or in a plastic bag with a rolling pin, until reduced to a medium-fine consistency; this should yield about ⅔ cup. Toss the crumbs with the grated Parmesan and the chopped parsley. Scatter the crumbs over the shrimp, pressing them in gently to adhere.

Bake for 8 to 10 minutes, or until the shrimp are nearly cooked though (timing can vary based on size of shrimp; do not overcook). Remove from the oven. With a rack about 5 inches from the heat source, preheat the broiler. Place the dish, on its baking sheet, under the broiler and broil until the crumbs are lightly browned, about 30 seconds. Place the parsley sprigs in the center of the dish, and lime or lemon wedges at the edge. Serve hot.

She ate them with her hands, just like everyone else.
> —*A Joe's captain to a TV news reporter, as*
> *Princess Caroline of Monaco was leaving the restaurant by limousine*

Jesse had told me about this wonderful restaurant, and big hotel, and this flowery story. So we picked up Jo Ann at summer camp in the Catskills ("He arrived with the most beautiful woman," Jo Ann said), and came down to Miami.

Everything was a mess. The place had been closed for the summer season, and a hurricane had just been through. I remember a big pot, and the mashed potatoes had been left in there for three months; they were so hard they just adhered to the pot. So we just threw pots and everything else away.

From this point in the story, Grace and Jo Ann both share their memories:

Grace: *Now, Jo Ann was only about thirteen, and I was still in my twenties. Of course, Jo Ann and I were competing for this man, and we didn't get along. No, we didn't get along at all. And Papa, of course, played both of us, because he didn't want to let go of either one.*

Jo Ann: *So many women had come into my life, and I never knew when the current one was leaving. So I really didn't like any of them because I figured, "Well, you'll be gone."*

Grace: *So it took years until everybody realized that everybody was here to stay.*

Jo Ann: *Grace is really the only mother I've ever known.*

Getting the restaurant back in shape wasn't easy. "There was no credit," Grace remembered all too well:

Because when we came back, there was a bushel basket full of bills. Do you know what a $3,500 meat bill was in 1945? And that's what we owed. Papa owed a couple of heavyweight gamblers money.

And we went around to all of the dealers, and they looked at Jo Ann and me, these two kids who didn't know from anything. Today I'm amazed that anybody did it, but everyone was really good to us, and they said, "We'll give you a chance."

People told us, "Well, you've got to go into bankruptcy, and pay ten cents on the dollar." And we said, "No, we won't do that. Everybody gets all of their money, and that's it."

And we paid everybody everything that was coming to them, one hundred percent on the dollar. It took us a few years, because we didn't have anything. There were about twelve coffee cups in this big restaurant. So when we came back, we had to start from scratch.

EAT AT JOE'S

Today, Joe and Jennie Weiss still have a place at Joe's—high above the main dining room is their photo, taken in 1918 outside their house.

This was also when Joe's got a new name. The restaurant was still called simply "Joe's Restaurant." Jo Ann explained: "The real reason it changed was because Daddy had given an ex-wife power of attorney when he was in the service. So instead of his trying to get back power of attorney, it was easier just to change the name."

And so Joe's Stone Crab was born.

Historical Hallmark

At that point, the restaurant consisted of one dining room with a limited menu: stone crabs, Maryland fried chicken, corn fritters, apple pie. Grace added other fish items to the menu, and Jo Ann worked a full shift all through high school.

"We didn't do the business that we do today," Grace says, "but we seated about 180, and did a fairly good business. Even then, I remember the aisles being full."

As business increased steadily, Joe's kept outgrowing its quarters. In 1962, the east dining room was added. The waiters jokingly called it the "Gigi Room," after a bar in the Hotel Fountainebleau, and the name stuck. The Garden Room was added in 1983. And there are plans for a new, spacious entrance patio, to make the inevitable long waits for a table more pleasant. Joe's was declared a Miami Beach historical hallmark by the City Council in 1975.

Everyone came to Joe's, and still does today. One of the reasons is that Joe's staff goes out of their way to let everyone enjoy their meals in peace. Grace Weiss said, "We never allowed people to go over with autograph books and carry on. Many restaurant owners will call the press, and allow people to bother celebrities, and we sort of protected everybody we could."

This photo of Joe DiMaggio eating at Joe's appeared in the *Miami Herald* in 1955.

Jo Ann: Joe DiMaggio would come, Mickey Mantle, all those people came to Joe's. Now Joe Louis, the fighter, was another story. Papa said, "Look, do you want me to keep the people away?" And he said, "No, these are my people, let them come."

The New Generation

Starting in the late 1960s, Joe's owned its own fisheries, so the restaurant could be assured of a constant supply of top-quality stone crabs. Jo Ann and her then-husband, Irwin "Say" Sawitz, ran the business together for several years. Though they are now divorced, Say runs the stone crabs operation, which supplies restaurants throughout the country, and Jo Ann (now blissfully remarried to Dr. Bob Bass) has been totally in charge since 1985. (At the entrance to Joe's, there is a photo of Jo Ann as a young girl, smiling in the courtyard. She still has the same sunny smile she did then; a recent magazine profile called her "a splendid brunette in expensive beige.")

A food lover whose curiosity has taken her to far-flung parts of the world, Jo Ann Bass is responsible for introducing many new dishes on the menu, including such Joe's classics as Creamed Garlic Spinach, Grilled Stuffed Tomatoes, and the addictive Cottage Fried Sweets—sweet potatoes sliced tissue-thin and fried, they're the best potato chips you ever tasted.

Joe's has been offered blandishments over the years, to open other branches, for franchises, for every imaginable (and highly lucrative) sort of business deal. But Jo Ann Bass, granddaughter of Joe Weiss and daughter of Jesse, is firm in her resolve to keep Joe's a single-family operation. "I'm death on another restaurant," she says. "Unless you're on top of everything twenty-four hours a day, sloppiness and mediocrity sets in."

Jo Ann runs Joe's, with over two hundred employees, like a benevolent mother hen. She knows every staff member, many of whom have been with Joe's for twenty, thirty, even forty years. And she instituted an employee profit-sharing plan that's one of the most generous in the industry.

A low-key dynamo, Jo Ann is everywhere in the restaurant, tasting sauces in the kitchen, arranging repairs, planning private parties, listening to employee problems, giving customers directions to the restaurant on the phone. "Jo Ann mops the floor and cleans the bathrooms if she sees they need it," says one family member.

When the dining room is full, with crowds in bibs contentedly dipping their crabs in mustard sauce, Jo Ann stops by to greet them as old friends (which many are).

And the fourth generation is well in place. Stephen Sawitz and Jodi Hershey Koganovsky, Jo Ann and Say's two children, both deftly handle managerial roles. A graduate of Cornell's School of Hotel and Restaurant Administration, Stephen is mostly out front; Jodi, like her mother, prefers to work behind the scenes and has a hand in several aspects of the business: the kitchen, dining room, take-away, shipping, and Stone Crabs, Inc., the fisheries arm.

Barbecued Alaska Salmon

On a trip to Alaska, Jo Ann Bass enjoyed salmon grilled outdoors. "That was the best salmon I ever had in my life," she said. "Adapting a recipe in *The Great American Seafood Cookbook* by Susan Herrmann Loomis, I came up with this, and we've been serving it at Joe's ever since." Originally, this was cooked on a charcoal grill, which works beautifully with salmon's fatty flesh. See the note below for instructions.

SERVES 4

Fish
4 6- to 8-ounce salmon fillets

Marinade
2 tablespoons soy sauce
1 teaspoon sake or sherry
Pinch of cayenne pepper
1 teaspoon Tabasco sauce
1 teaspoon Worcestershire sauce
1 tablespoon dry white wine
1 teaspoon fresh lemon juice
1 teaspoon minced fresh ginger
1/2 teaspoon sugar
2 garlic cloves, minced

Sauce
4 tablespoons unsalted butter
1/4 cup packed brown sugar
2 teaspoons fresh lemon juice
2 teaspoons dry white wine
1 large garlic clove, minced
1/4 teaspoon Tabasco sauce
1/3 cup minced onion
Salt
Pinch of cayenne pepper

Lime or lemon wedges,
 for garnish

Rinse the salmon fillets and pat dry. Remove as many bones as possible. Cut 2 or 3 shallow slashes in each skin side, without cutting all the way through.

Make the marinade: Combine all the ingredients in a mixing bowl. Place the salmon, flesh side down, in a shallow nonaluminum dish. Pour in the marinade, cover with plastic wrap, and refrigerate for 1 to 2 hours, turning the salmon over once or twice.

Preheat the broiler, with a rack about 5 inches from the heat.

Make the sauce: Melt the butter in a small saucepan over medium heat. Stir in the brown sugar. Add all of the remaining sauce ingredients and cook until well mixed.

Place the salmon in an ovenproof skillet; stir a tablespoon or two of water into the marinade and pour it around the fish. Place the skillet on a stovetop burner over medium heat. Cover the pan and bring to a simmer. Lower the heat and simmer gently for 2 minutes.

Spoon the sauce mixture over the salmon; cover and simmer for 2 minutes longer.

Now uncover the pan and place it directly under the broiler. Broil for 2 to 3 minutes, or until the fish is glazed and just firm when touched gently with a fingertip. With a spatula, transfer the salmon fillets to warm serving plates. Pour a little of the pan juices over and around the fish and serve hot. Garnish with lime or lemon wedges.

Grilling Note

To grill the salmon, prepare a hot charcoal fire or preheat a gas grill. Place the fish on a sheet of aluminum foil that is about 2 inches larger on all sides than the salmon. (The aluminum foil should not cover the entire grill; the smoke should be able to come up and around it. Susan Loomis's original recipe used a 2- to 3-pound salmon fillet in one piece. You can do it that way, or place 4 individual portions on the foil.) Place the foil on the grill. Pour any marinade left in the dish over the salmon.

Cover the grill, leaving the vents open. Cook for 5 minutes.

Uncover the grill and pour ¼ cup of the sauce over the salmon. Cover and cook for 5 minutes. Repeat the process, using the remaining sauce. Cook for 2 minutes longer, or until salmon is just cooked through.

I've been here twenty-two years. I love it. I think it's a family here—if you have a problem, you can talk to somebody. You're not just a number; you're a person here, and that's what makes the difference. When I came here, if we did 800 dinners on a Saturday night, it was a great night. Now, when we do 1,400, we're slow. It's a fun place to work.

—Judy Goupee, head cashier

Whether you're a dishwasher or the maitre d', Jo Ann treats you the same.

—Lori Kahn, Jo Ann's secretary

> **I**f I was convicted and put in the chair, and asked what my last meal would be, it would be Joe's stone crabs. And I better have a pretty good plateful!
>
> —Al Martino

One major change was the opening of Joe's Take Away in 1987. This runaway success is overseen by Stephen, Jodi, and manager Lisa Rosati. Also, since the mid-1980s, Osaka Joe's and Tokyo Joe's have been going strong in Japan. While Joe's does not own these operations, the restaurant is their supplier of stone crabs, chowder, and Key lime pie, as well as the technology.

While quality is never easy to achieve in the restaurant business, it's all the more remarkable when you consider the size of Joe's operation. It's one thing to put out one or two hundred fine meals per night, but to keep the quality high is something else entirely.

James T. Jones, Anthony Arneson, and Rose McDaniel get ready for another busy lunch.

Rose and Dick McDaniel remember getting a call from Jo Ann and Say one night during the late Sixties. "That night, the restaurant had twelve hundred for dinner," Dick says, "breaking the record. Everyone had champagne—it was just awesome." That record has since been broken, many times over. On December 29, 1989, Joe's served 686 for lunch and 1,956 for dinner.

Today, Joe's serves some 2,000 pounds of stone crabs per day in season—15,000 pounds per week. Joe's Stone Crab is now one of the half-dozen highest-grossing independent restaurants in the country. And that's based on a seven-month season, as compared with a twelve-month season by all the others. Lisa Rosati puts it succinctly: "Our success is our simplicity, and the consistency."

And what about Jodi's kids—will they be the fifth generation to run Joe's Stone Crab? "I have great designs for them," Jo Ann says. "But I don't want them to miss their childhood."

Having grown up in the business, and now carrying it, with his mother and sister, into the future, Stephen Sawitz says, "Mom has a good handle on the wheel; she's

40

steering the ship, and she knows what she's doing. Joe's runs us, and we run it. It's hard to believe there were crabs in the water when this was just a fish shack, and no one knew they had been there, and for how long. It was just an accident, a real accident! I don't care who runs Joe's. Mother Nature is the ultimate card holder."

In October 1985, after an article about Joe's appeared in the *Miami Herald*, Joe's received this letter:

I saw the article in the Miami Herald, *I was surprised to see the date 1930.*

1926 as a 16-year-old boy, I worked at the Roman Pools—across from the Roney Plaza. Mr. Joe Weiss was there one afternoon—and gave me cards to give to customers about his place.

A week later he hired me to work evenings at his place.

It was a small white house with 10 tables. There was a picture in there with Mr. and Mrs. and myself. We had on long white aprons—wonder if it's still around. I worked 1926, 1927, 1928, then left for California.

You mention Al Capone. How about these names—Ralph Bunche—diplomat; Thomas Dewey—governor; James Michener—writer; Percy Strauss—Macy's dept. store owner; Bamberger family—Newark dept. store owner; Joe Kennedy with Gloria Swanson and Anna May Wong, movie people.

However, the best customers were brought to Joe's place by a Col. Bradley...of Bradley's Casino. They would come down around 11 o'clock in 3 white convertible Packards, 7 to a car—I would get a $30 tip, and Mr. Joe would get a $50 tip. This would be 3 nights out of a week.

I saved my money to go to Hollywood, Cal. Joe spent his playing "clubiash"—a Jewish card game.

I hope this little message will be accepted by you in good intent.

As I will be 77 Nov. 28, and the article brought back many fond memories.

Mayberry Kohut

P.S. I spent my winters working at Mike Romanoff's Place in Hollywood, Cal.

I've worked at restaurants all over the United States. Joe's is the only family I've worked for that takes care of their help. I met Stephen when I worked at Cye's Rivergate; he was working there one summer when he was in college, and we hit it off. Stephen told his grandfather Jesse that I would make a good waiter, and he brought me in. I love it. Every day, more and more, I love it. That's why I'm working eight shifts a week.

—Eddie Rolle, waiter

Joe's Apple Pie

This is an extraordinary pie, developed by Jo Ann Bass. It's piled high with apples and topped with a brown sugar streusel. At Joe's, these are baked every day by Esther Salinas; on weekends, she bakes about two dozen pies, plus more for the Take Away.

MAKES ONE 9 1/2- OR 10-INCH PIE

Pie Pastry
2 cups all-purpose flour
1 tablespoon plus 1 teaspoon sugar
1/2 teaspoon salt
1/2 cup cold unsalted butter, cut into pieces
1/4 cup plus 2 tablespoons solid vegetable shortening
1 tablespoon white vinegar
2 tablespoons cold water, or more as needed

Filling
8 red apples (Northern Spy, Jonathan, Macoun)
Juice of 1/2 lemon

1/2 cup sugar, or more to taste, depending on sweetness of apples
3 tablespoons flour
1 1/2 teaspoons cinnamon
1/2 teaspoon cloves
1/2 teaspoon nutmeg
1/2 teaspoon salt

Topping
1 cup plus 2 tablespoons flour
1 stick plus 1 1/2 tablespoons cold unsalted butter, cut into chunks
2/3 cup dark brown sugar
1/2 cup pecans, broken up coarsely

For the pastry: In a food processor or medium bowl, mix the flour, sugar, and salt briefly. Add the butter and shortening and cut the ingredients together until crumbly. Combine the vinegar and water; add to the mixture, mixing briefly. If necessary, add just enough cold water for the dough to come together. Gather it into a ball; then wrap in plastic wrap and chill for at least 1/2 hour.

On a lightly floured surface, roll the dough out fairly thin into a neat circle. Fit it, without stretching, into a buttered deep 9½- or 10-inch pie pan. Form a high fluted border. Chill the pie shell.

For the filling: Peel, quarter, and core the apples and slice them into a large mixing bowl, tossing them with the lemon juice to prevent darkening. In a small bowl, stir together the sugar, flour, cinnamon, cloves, nutmeg, and salt.

42

Sprinkle this mixture over the apples and toss to coat.

Preheat the oven to 375°F.

For the topping: In a food processor, or using two knives or your fingers, cut together the flour and butter, leaving the butter in pieces about the size of a nickel. Mix in the brown sugar, then the pecans. Refrigerate the mixture.

Scatter the apple mixture into the crust, mounding it in the center. Place in the oven; place a sheet of aluminum foil on the rack below to catch any drips. Bake for 25 minutes.

Raise the oven heat to 400°F. Scatter the topping over the apples, covering them completely and pressing gently to adhere. Bake until the topping is nicely browned, 25 to 30 minutes longer. Cool the pie on a wire rack; serve at room temperature or lukewarm.

Esther Salinas bakes Joe's Apple Pie fresh every day.

Filling Key lime pies.

ey Lime Pie

Jo Ann Bass has *never* given out this recipe; customers have been known to offer substantial sums for it, to no avail.

Paul Wilson Sr., who has been at Joe's since 1955, bakes eighty to one hundred Key lime pies a day, six days a week. "They call me Daddy," Paul says. "I'm the one and only one who bakes these pies. I start at six in the morning, and I finish at around ten." Every day, he has some 200 egg whites left over, which Joe's trades with a local bakery for day-old egg bread, which is used for the bread pudding sold at the Take Away.

"This pie is the best one, the number one," Daddy says, taking twenty-five of them out of the oven to cool. "I have people come from miles around to try these pies. They say there's no pie like Joe's. That's because it's not the same man making 'em. Here at Joe's, you get real quality.

"I can't give out the secret. The recipe is not given out. If I gave out the recipe, we'd find these pies somewhere else. That recipe is behind the iron curtain. I've got to look out for my job, and the people I work for. They take care of mine, and I take care of them. These pies go all over the world—even to Tokyo. We send the ones I make over to Japan by the thousands."

This is Richard's re-creation of Daddy's original, based on repeated tries.

MAKES 1 9-INCH PIE

Graham Cracker Crust
1 wax paper–wrapped package graham crackers (1/3 of a 1-pound box) or 1 cup plus 2 1/2 tablespoons graham cracker crumbs
5 tablespoons melted unsalted butter
1/3 cup sugar

Filling
3 egg yolks
Grated zest of 2 limes (about 1 1/2 teaspoons)

1 14-ounce can sweetened condensed milk
2/3 cup freshly squeezed lime juice (if you can get Key limes, use them; otherwise use regular limes)

Topping
1 cup heavy or whipping cream, chilled
3 tablespoons confectioners' sugar

For the graham cracker crust: Preheat the oven to 350°F. Butter a 9-inch pie pan. Break up the graham crackers; place in a food processor and process to crumbs. (If you don't have a food processor, place the crackers in a large plastic bag; seal and then crush the crackers with a rolling pin.) Add the melted butter and sugar and pulse or stir until combined. Press the mixture into the bottom and sides of the pie pan, forming a neat border around the edge. Bake the crust until set and golden, 8 minutes. Set aside on a wire rack; leave the oven on.

For the filling: Meanwhile, in an electric mixer with the wire whisk attachment, beat the egg yolks and lime zest at high speed until very fluffy, about 5 minutes. Gradually add the condensed milk and continue to beat until thick, 3 or 4 minutes longer. Lower the mixer speed and slowly add the lime juice, mixing just until combined, no longer. Pour the mixture into the crust. Bake for 10 minutes, or until the filling has just set. Cool on a wire rack, then refrigerate. Freeze for 15 to 20 minutes before serving.

For the topping: Whip the cream and the confectioners' sugar until nearly stiff. Cut the pie in wedges and serve very cold, topping each wedge with a

OPPOSITE: Paul "Daddy" Wilson Sr. beams as he whisks away another masterpiece.

HOW KEY LIME PIE GOT ON JOE'S MENU...BY ACCIDENT

Second to stone crabs, Key lime pie is the dish for which Joe's is known. But it wasn't always that way. Grace Weiss remembers that about thirty years ago, "there was a writer from the *Chicago Sun-Times*. He wrote in a syndicated column that he had been to Miami, and had the best Key lime pie he ever ate at Joe's. Well, Joe's didn't even make Key lime pie—all we had was apple pie. I don't know where he had that Key lime pie, but the article ran all over the United States. So Jo Ann made this little Key lime pie at home. She finagled around to make it on a large scale, and that's how it got onto the menu." In 1978, the *Miami Herald's* restaurant critic declared that Joe's Key lime pie was "the paradigm of that South Florida staple against which all other Key lime pies should be measured."

They call me Daddy. I treat the younger ones like I do my own. I had my son, Paul Jr., working here on weekends when he was still in school. Now, he makes the chowder and the hash browns. My baby son, Larry, used to work here, but now he's in management at Epicure, a Miami Beach gourmet market. He's like us—he's got a home there.

—Paul Wilson Sr.

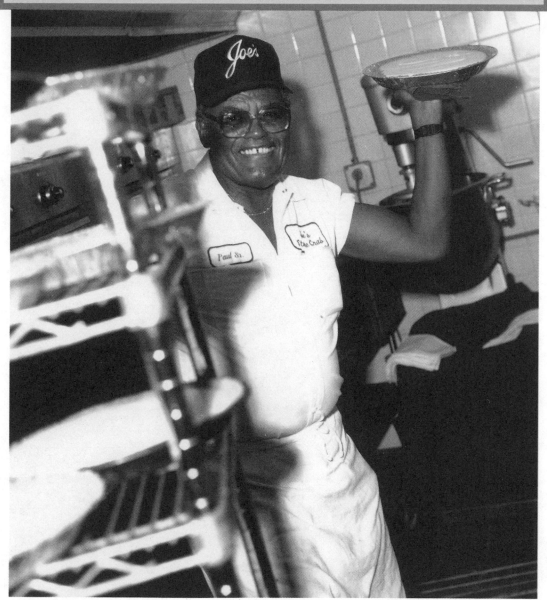

The Stone Crab Story

For

decades, residents of and visitors to Miami have known that stone crabs *(Menippe mercenaria)* are, as one local crabber puts it, "Florida's unique delicacy." But it wasn't always that way. Thanks to the ichthyologist who was doing research on local marine life, Joe Weiss discovered the delicacy by accident. Before that, those who had tried to cook and eat the crabs as you would other types of crab—boiled and eaten hot—had been disappointed in the flavor.

The secret, it turned out, was chilling the meaty claws immediately after boiling them. Eaten cold, the flesh is firm and sweet. "You wouldn't dream of eating them any other way," says Richard McDaniel, chief crab inspector at Joe's, who himself ran fisheries for several years.

PREVIOUS PAGES: The Tom Thumb Market on the corner of 14th and Washington; INSET: Miami Beach Chamber of Commerce, circa 1930. ABOVE: Grading crab claws at the fishery.

Mature stone crabs are 50 percent claw by weight: "Like Popeye—all arms," McDaniel says. During the 1960s, conservation laws stipulated that only the claws could be harvested; they're detached from the wide bodies, and the bodies, which contain little meat, are thrown back into the water. In two years, the claws will regenerate to a length of 2¾ inches, which is the minimum legal size for harvesting. (You can remove any part of a crab's body, except the eyes, and it will regenerate. Also, crabs can reproduce while growing new claws.)

The best stone crabs, according to one veteran in the business, are from the Florida Gulf coast. There are also New England stone crabs called Jonah crabs; Georgia stone crabs, Texas-Louisiana stone crabs, Mexican stone crabs; Chile, Peru, Ecuador stone crabs. Irish and English stone crabs are green. On the West Coast, it's called a red crab, but it is a stone crab.

One year, there was a crab shortage. "There was not a stone crab in the state of Florida," Grace Weiss recalls. "We had to bring in *cangrejos morros* from Cuba, by air. They would arrive packed in seaweed, and we used to dump them out in the alley, and

50

we'd run around trying to catch them."

Before conservation, crabs were always brought to the restaurant alive and whole, in burlap bags. "They'd dump them out on the floor," one employee remembers, "and go chase 'em, and boil them alive, just like a Maine lobster. Then they'd chill them, take the claws off, and throw the bodies away. That was done for years."

Jo Ann Bass says that when Joe Weiss first started serving stone crabs, "that was the start of the stone crab industry. That has put it into the culinary encyclopedia. I'm sure eventually somebody would have done it, but my grandparents *did* do it."

Getting Stone Crabs Out of the Water

"All crabbers get bitten," says Dick McDaniel, who oversees crabs for Joe's. "I've even been bitten by the claws. You've seen a chicken running around with its head chopped off? Well, a stone crab claw still has reactions left in it, even though it's been removed from its body.

"The crab exerts pressure with its claw; it gets a tighter and tighter grip until its prey finally breaks open. So its strength is unbelievable." With one claw, the crab can exert thirteen to fifteen thousand pounds of pressure per square inch; crabs easily crush oyster shells to bits.

Florida stone crabs are found in southwestern Florida, down in the Keys and all along the Gulf of Mexico coast. When Joe Weiss first started serving them, they were plentiful in Miami, but the waters were dredged as Miami boomed in the 1920s, and the stone crabs moved south.

Dick McDaniel describes the crabbing process.

Crab fishing requires back-breaking labor. Crabbers head out in boats well before dawn. Their boats are loaded with a thousand pounds of fresh fish heads for bait, because stone crabs are very particular. The captain heads out into open sea with a crew of one to three men. They can fish anywhere from a mile offshore to ninety miles out, where the water is ninety feet deep. You go to where the crabs are walking; you move your lines to where the activity is.

You try to time it so you get to the first trap, attached to a buoy, at first light. You pull the first trap, which is connected to the buoy by eighty or ninety feet of rope. You pull the buoy up to the boat and put it on a pulley that is connected to a motor; the pulley is doing

The size of a claw is usually judged by hand, but a scale is sometimes used to make a tough call.

the work. The trap is a square 16 x 16-inch box made of wood slats; as soon as the trap breaks the water, you pull it up and put it on the gunnel, or gunwale. The crabs get in by climbing up the side of the trap; they walk into a hole and drop down in. They can't swim—they only walk—so they can't get out. Each trap can hold ten or twelve crabs. Sometimes the trap is full; sometimes you get one or two, or none.

You take the trap up and take the crabs out. You've got to be fast. Compared to human reactions, crabs are slow, but you can still get bitten. So you reach in, pull him out, and put him in a crab crawl, a wooden pen on the boat that holds live crabs on wet burlap. The crabbers wear cotton gloves with plastic dots on them—up to three pairs at a time—and they go through dozens of pairs each week, protection against sharp barnacles as well as crabs.

The fish bones—which are also sharp—are then taken out of the trap and the trap is scrubbed. Now you've got to get fresh bait in the trap, close the lid, lock the locks, throw it overboard, and spool out the line ninety feet so the trap won't get tangled up and sink. You have to put them out in order along the line. So it's timing—you pull, throw, pull, throw, pull, throw. Your productivity is measured by your efficiency. There's no time to waste in between.

A good crabber can pull a thousand traps a day—by sundown. And this is back-breaking physical work. Backbreaking. The traps weigh a ton, the men are getting soaking wet with saltwater, scraped by sharp barnacles, bounced around on the boat in rough water, and the captain is speeding up to get to the next trap, while you're breathing diesel exhaust. You're wearing rubber aprons and boots, but you're soaking wet. You see a crab puller at the end of the day, you're looking at one worn-out puppy. There's no such thing as a lazy crab puller. In stone crabbing, most guys are burned out by their late forties.

Now, the boat steams toward home. And all the men start shucking crabs. They reach into the crawl, pull out a live crab, and break off one or two claws, whichever are legal size—2¾ inches—and throw the crab body overboard.

The claws go into boxes or bags, and the boat is hosed down for the next day. The boat pulls into the fish house; cranes start lifting the bags of claws overboard.

Jo Ann Bass, in a rare moment of pride, describes why stone crabs at Joe's aren't like those anywhere else: "Some people say that you can get stone crabs anywhere, but I think the ones at Joe's are unique. First, there are the controls, starting with the processing at our own fisheries and continuing through with the handling. And then there's the careful cracking at the restaurant."

Baskets, each holding a hundred pounds of claws, are lifted onto scales and the claws are weighed and recorded. The claws now go into the cooking room. It's important not to let the claws get too cold before they're cooked or the meat will stick to the shells.

The claws are boiled in galvanized steel baskets. An electric hoist lowers five hundred pounds at a time into water-filled stainless steel tanks, where pipes inject live steam to boil the water very rapidly—about two hundred gallons of fresh ice water comes to a full boil in under thirty minutes. From the time the boiling water returns to a boil, the claws cook for eight minutes. Then they're taken out of the boiling water and immersed in a chilling tank filled with ice water. By the time the next basket is cooked, the previous batch of claws is ice-cold.

The crab claws, still in their wheeled baskets, are then iced down with shaved ice to keep them cold (but not frozen) and wheeled into a walk-in cooler with fans blowing cold air. At the end of the night, usually by midnight, the door is closed and locked, and the cooking room hosed down.

The next morning, the crab claws are washed and graded for size. Experienced people know a large from a medium by feel, but they do use an electronic scale. ("For what we call 'maybes,' " Dick says. "Maybe it's big, maybe it isn't.") The catch is recorded by size.

The claws are then packed in boxes, marked for inventory, stacked, put on trucks, and shipped to Joe's in Miami Beach. "Because we're dealing with our own fisheries, we know that they're handled correctly every step of the way. And that makes all the difference in the quality of the product."

Top: Instructions on cracking crabs come with every Take Away order. Above: Manuel "Freddy" Pagan will crack your crabs for you at the restaurant.

Stone Crabs in the Restaurant

Each day, Dick McDaniel explains, Joe's Stone Crab knows how many pounds they need: for lunch, for dinner, for the Take Away. The trucks arrive at Joe's early in the morning, sometimes by 4 A.M. When the restaurant crew arrives at 6:30, they take the crabs off the eighteen-wheelers, still in their original containers. Then, with a forklift, they put twenty-five boxes—about two thousand pounds—on a pallet, and move them into the refrigerated crab room. It's something to see on an eighty-degree day in Miami Beach—kitchen workers with parkas driving forklifts stacked high with boxes of crab claws through the kitchen.

On a good day, Joe's brings in five thousand pounds of crab claws. They're still on shaved ice, and they're kept cold until they're served. So the crabs served today at lunch were just pulled out of the water the night before and brought to the restaurant kitchen that morning.

In the old days, they used to cook the crabs in the restaurant. Today those same cooking baskets are used to to cook potatoes for hash browns.

Two men at lunch and three men at dinner do nothing but crack crab claws at special cracking tables. Using a wooden mallet with an aluminum face, each man cracks the three joints of the claw in an unvarying rhythm: pa-pa-PA pa-pa-PA.

"Three whacks," says one seasoned practitioner: "End knuckle, middle knuckle, claw." They make it look easy, but it's similar to diamond cutting: a quick motion, but if you're not precise . . .

ABOVE: In the early years at Joe's (circa 1930), Jesse Weiss rolls up his sleeves and joins in cracking crabs.
LEFT: Even after many years at the top of the restaurant business, Jesse still finds time to get into the kitchen. He always could crack crabs just right.

"AN ILL-CRACKED STONE CRAB IS A TORMENT ON THE DAMNED."
—CRAIG CLAIBORNE

The trick to cracking a crab," McDaniel explains, "is the same in theory as cracking an egg—you want to crack the shell, so you can pull it apart and take the meat out. You don't want to splinter it and drive the pieces into the meat. You want to hit not too hard, but not too lightly. A table lasts us almost a season; we go through hundreds of mallets each season." The cracked claws are then arranged on oval platters, piled in a pyramid shape, with all the black tips lined up, looking magnificent. In the early days of Joe's, they went for seventy-five cents an order.

French-Fried Eggplant

SERVES 6

1 medium eggplant
2 eggs
2 tablespoons cold water
½ teaspoon salt
⅔ cup all-purpose flour
1¼ cups seasoned dry bread
  crumbs, or as needed

2 tablespoons chopped fresh
  parsley
4 cups vegetable oil, or as needed
  for deep-frying
Lemon wedges, for serving
  (optional)

Peel the eggplant with a paring knife. Cut it crosswise into rounds about ¾-inch thick. Now cut each round into strips about ¾-inch wide.

Set up breading: Beat the egg with the water and salt in a shallow bowl. Next to this, place the flour in a pie plate or shallow bowl. Combine the bread crumbs and parsley in a third pie plate or shallow bowl.

Dip the eggplant strips into the egg mixture. Lift them out with a skimmer, draining off excess, and dip them into the flour. Shake off excess flour and dip them back into the egg wash. Now dip them into the bread crumbs, coating them well. Lift them out, shaking off excess crumbs, and place on a wax paper–lined baking sheet. Refrigerate for at least ½ hour to set the breading.

Heat the oil in a deep skillet or casserole to a temperature of 350 to 360°F. When the oil reaches 350°F, a pinch of flour will sizzle energetically as as it hits the oil; a cube of bread will turn golden in about 30 seconds. Adjust the heat to maintain a steady temperature. Fry the eggplant until golden brown, turning them once, about 3 minutes. Drain well and keep warm while you fry the remaining eggplant. Serve hot.

Herbed Rice Pilaf

This recipe was developed by Bob Bass, Jo Ann's husband. It goes well with any fish or seafood dish.

SERVES 6

1 tablespoon unsalted butter
1 small onion, chopped
1 carrot, peeled and chopped
2 garlic cloves, minced
2 teaspoons candied orange peel, or the grated zest of 1 small orange
1 tablespoon Spice Mix (recipe follows)
1 1/2 cups raw long-grain white rice

1 1/2 teaspoons salt, or to taste
1/2 teaspoon pepper
1 1/2 cups cups chicken broth
1 cup water
2 plum tomatoes, cored, seeded, and diced
3 tablespoons slivered almonds, toasted until lightly golden
2 tablespoons chopped fresh parsley

Heat the butter in a heavy saucepan over medium heat. Add the onion and carrot and sauté, tossing, for 4 or 5 minutes. Add the garlic, orange peel, Spice Mixture, rice, and salt and pepper. Sauté, stirring, for 2 minutes longer.

Add the broth and water and bring to a boil. Reduce heat to low, cover, and simmer for 16 minutes. Add the tomatoes and simmer 2 minutes longer. Virtually all of the liquid should be absorbed; if it is not, raise the heat slightly and cook, uncovered, stirring, until it is. Turn off the heat and let the rice sit, uncovered, for about 5 minutes. Correct the seasonings and serve hot, sprinkled with the almonds and parsley.

SPICE MIX

3 teaspoons cumin seed
3 teaspoons turmeric
2 teaspoons cinnamon

1 teaspoon allspice
1 teaspoon dried thyme
1/2 teaspoon cayenne pepper

Toast the cumin seed in a small dry skillet over medium-low heat until fragrant, about 5 minutes. Place it in a spice mill with the other spices and grind until powdery. Store in a tightly closed jar.

Sautéed Shrimp in Garlic Butter

SERVES 2

2 tablespoons Garlic Butter
(recipe follows)
16 to 18 medium-large shrimp
(12 to 16 ounces), peeled but
with tails on, and deveined

All-purpose flour
Lime or lemon wedges, for
garnish

Put the butter in a large skillet, preferably nonstick, over medium heat.

Place the flour in a pie plate or shallow soup bowl. Toss the shrimp in the flour to coat lightly, shaking off excess. Place in the hot butter without crowding (work in batches if necessary). Sauté, turning once or twice, until the shrimp are just pink but not browned, 1 to 2 minutes total. Serve hot, garnished with lime or lemon wedges.

GARLIC BUTTER

2 tablespoons unsalted butter
2 garlic cloves, crushed with a

knife blade and peeled,
but left whole

Heat the butter and garlic in a large nonstick skillet over medium-low heat. Cook, stirring now and then, until the garlic is fragrant and beginning to brown lightly, about 3 minutes. Remove and discard the garlic.

Perhaps the difficulty of obtaining a stone crab dinner has contributed to the exclusiveness of Menippe in the halls of Lucullus. Only through the Florida Keys can he be caught in this country, and only in the Miami area can he be properly prepared for the table. True, [Sherman] Billingsley has an airplane shipment of claws sent to him in New York now and again, but they are marked for the palates of bosom friends, and even the most treasured customer of Sherman's New York eatery [The Stork Club] cannot bribe him to part with even a single nut-sweet pincer.

—*Bruce Henry, "The Gentry Eats Crabs,"* Esquire, *February 1939*

Shrimp Louis

This is a good-looking cold plate. The Louis dressing can be used for other cold seafood, too.

SERVES 2

3/4 pound baby or medium-
  size shrimp
Salt
Juice of 1 small lime
Lettuce leaves
1 cup cooked garbanzo beans

1 large ripe tomato, cored
  and sliced
2 hard-cooked eggs
2 lemons, cut in half crosswise
8 ripe black olives
4 thin round slices green
  bell pepper

Drop the shrimp into boiling water flavored with a little salt and lime juice; cook just until pink, usually 1 to 2 minutes. Drain and cool slightly; shell and devein. Place in a bowl; cover with plastic wrap and chill.

Arrange lettuce leaves to cover two large dinner plates; at Joe's, this is made on large oval plates. Place a mound of shrimp at one side, a mound of garbanzo beans on the other. Place tomato slices in the four "corners" of the plate. Cut the eggs lengthwise in quarters; place a quarter next to each tomato slice. Place a lemon half at the end of each plate, and 2 olives at the top and bottom. Place the green pepper rings at the edges. Cover and chill if not serving immediately. Serve the dressing on the side, in a small sauceboat.

LOUIS DRESSING

MAKES ABOUT 2/3 CUP

1/2 cup mayonnaise
2 tablespoons chili sauce
1 tablespoon grated onion
1 tablespoon chopped fresh parsley
Salt and pepper

1 tablespoon heavy cream, or
  more as needed
1/4 teaspoon Worcestershire
  sauce, or to taste
Several drops Tabasco sauce

Combine all dressing ingredients; stir until blended. Chill, covered, until serving time. If too thick, stir in a little more cream.

Broiled Fish with Garlic Butter

Pedro Morales and Eugene "Blue Jay" Green are the chief fish cooks; they've been with Joe's for forty and twenty-two years, respectively. During dinner, they have many orders going at a time but manage to pull each piece of fish from the fire at just the right moment. This easy restaurant method, with a small amount of water in the pan, keeps the fish moist as it broils.

SERVES 2

2 fish steaks (swordfish, tuna, salmon) or thick fish fillets (cod, scrod, halibut), 6 to 8 ounces each
Salt
1/4 teaspoon paprika

1 1/2 teaspoons unsalted butter, cut into small pieces
2 tablespoons warm Garlic Butter (page 58)
Lime or lemon wedges, for garnish

Preheat the broiler, with the rack about 5 inches from the heat source. Rinse and dry the fish. Place the fish in a pie plate or other shallow heat-proof dish. Sprinkle with salt and paprika, then dot with butter. Pour enough water around the fish so that it sits in about 3/8 inch of liquid.

Broil, without turning, until the fish is lightly golden and is just firm when pressed gently with a fingertip, about 8 minutes. (Timing can vary; allow 8 to 10 minutes per inch of thickness.)

With a slotted spatula, transfer the fish to warm serving plates, letting the liquid drain off. Drizzle the Garlic Butter over each serving. Garnish with lime or lemon wedges and serve hot.

> **T**he crabs are as good as those of Brittany, which I thought were unique in the world. And the Key lime pie is as good as the crabs.
>
> —*Claude Jolly, food critic of* L'Express, *Paris, 1980, on Joe's Stone Crab*

STONE CRAB SIZES

Though the law imposes no regulation on the sizing of crabs, Joe's maintains its own standards for grading:

Medium: 8 per pound, about 2 ounces each

Large: 4 per pound, about 4 ounces each

Junior Jumbo: 5½–7 ounces each

Jumbo or Super Jumbo: 7–12 ounces each

Colossals: 12–8 ounces each

Cottage Fried Sweets

At Joe's, these are served on an oval plate lined with a cloth napkin. Cottage fried potatoes are done the same way; use Idaho potatoes instead.

SERVES 4

4 cups vegetable oil, or as needed for deep-frying

3 large sweet potatoes, peeled and sliced into rounds slightly less than 1/8-inch thick
Salt

Heat the oil in a deep skillet or casserole to a temperature of 350 to 360°F. When the oil reaches 350°F, a pinch of flour will sizzle energetically as it hits the oil; a cube of bread will turn golden in about 30 seconds. Adjust the heat as necessary to maintain a steady temperature.

Working in batches, fry the potatoes until crisp and beginning to turn lightly golden, about 3 minutes. Drain well on paper towels.

Now, working in batches, drop the potatoes back into the oil and fry briefly, 10 to 30 seconds, to crisp them up. Drain well on paper towels. Sprinkle with salt to taste, and serve immediately.

Shoestring Sweets

Shoestring potatoes are done this way, too; use Idaho potatoes instead.

SERVES 4

4 cups vegetable oil, or as needed for deep-frying

3 large sweet potatoes, peeled
Salt

Heat the oil in a deep skillet or casserole to a temperature of 350 to 360°F. Adjust the heat as necessary to maintain a steady temperature.

Cut the potatoes lengthwise into slices slightly less than 1/4-inch thick. Then cut each slice in strips slightly less than 1/4-inch wide. Working in batches, fry the potatoes until crisp and beginning to turn pale gold, about 3 minutes. Drain well on paper towels. Sprinkle with salt to taste, and serve immediately.

The classic Joe's feast: stone crab claws, melted butter, mustard sauce, hash browns, grilled stuffed tomatoes, creamed spinach, and cole slaw.

THE STONE CRAB STORY

Jesse Weiss

The Heart and Soul of Joe's Stone Crab

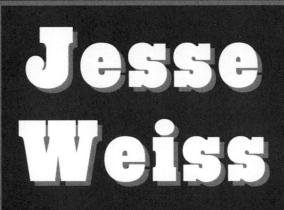

His

parents started Joe's, but Jesse Weiss was the key figure in consolidating the prominence the restaurant still enjoys.

"Jesse was a character," says one longtime Miami resident. "He was a scoundrel, a womanizer to the hundredth degree, a gambler. But everyone who came into Joe's wanted to see Jesse. He knew everyone—movie stars, journalists, politicians, sports people, gangsters. He would come by your table and it was a big deal. He was a Damon Runyon character." Runyon himself, not surprisingly, was a longtime friend of Jesse's.

"It was Papa's disposition that brought Joe's so many VIP's," says his wife, Grace. "Because he had that personality. And he never burdened them with anything but a gift of love."

Like all once-in-a-lifetime personalities, Jesse is almost impossible to describe (and some of the descriptions, while accurate, are hard to believe). But his own recollections, as well as those of his family and many friends, give a pretty fair idea of the man, who enjoys a place among legendary twentieth-century American restaurateurs.

Even as a boy, Jesse played by his own rules. He reminisces about going by ferry to school in Miami:

I was sort of a hell-raiser, but so were we all. During Prohibition, we'd watch bootleggers land here on the beach and then ship the stuff—the liquor—to Miami. One night, we stole a pint bottle of whiskey, and when we got on the ferry boat, we put it in front of the captain and he ran the boat into the ground! We were the only four passengers in the morning. So from then on, we kept our fishing tackle on the ferry, and we kept him supplied, and every day, we'd get that note [for school] . . . the rudder broke, or some other excuse. We had a very interesting year.

EAT AT JOE'S

"His heart was as big as the city of Miami Beach," says Allan Myerson, Joe's chief financial officer. "Any stranger who'd walk up to him and put the touch on him with the slightest bit of a sob story, Jesse's hand goes into the pocket and he'd give whatever was in there."

"At the same time," Jo Ann says, "Papa was really not terribly responsible. So it was like taking two steps forward and three backward. Mother would get some bills paid off, and the next thing we knew Papa had gambled away behind her back, and she would try to pay off the gambling debt." Jesse's wife, Grace, explains:

What he was doing was taking out the money and putting his bad checks in. He would get dressed in the morning, and go to the track with every dime that he had. He'd come back and sleep a couple hours, and then come down and have dinner, and greet everybody. Everybody loved Jesse. Even to this day. And of course, he chased women. I think every woman in America. And women loved him, because he was a good-time Charlie. He took them to the best places. And anyone that ever became angry with him, they never stayed mad.

Jo Ann: *Yes, Mother. Maybe it's my own romantic theory, but I think it has to be a great love affair between you and Daddy, because of what it went through—I mean, my father would stand at the front door, my mother was always in the back at the cash register, and name calling would resound across the dining room . . .*

Grace: *(Laughing) And throwing things . . .*

Jo Ann: *And many a time, I would be caught in the middle. Daddy never hit, but he would throw—pots, and pans . . .*

Grace: *He had a pretty good mouth on him.*

Jo Ann: *But it weathered all that, and your love is even stronger today . . .*

PREVIOUS PAGES: Jesse Weiss (left) and Arthur Godfrey; INSET: Guy Lombardo, Hy Gardner, and Jesse. OPPOSITE: Jesse in the friendly grip of Red Hot Mama Sophie Tucker. ABOVE: (top) Jesse with the lovely Terry Moore, (center) posing with his car in 1929, and (bottom) with Phil Donahue and Phyllis Diller in the 1970s.

JESSE WEISS

67

Jesse tells this one about himself:

One night I married a gal I met in a bar. We stopped in Fort Lauderdale and got married. You didn't have to wait three days. I woke up the next morning in a hotel in Palm Beach, and I saw this doll next to me. After she woke up I says, "Honey, I don't want to be rude. Is this a social call or a professional visit?" I didn't want to do the wrong thing. If she was a hooker, I wanted to take care of her. She said, "Neither one."

Bob Bass, Jo Ann's husband, tells this story:

My dad owned a jewelry store in downtown Miami for twenty years. Jesse knew my folks and came in and ordered seven gold and crystal desk clocks, one for each of the Miami Beach commissioners, and one for the mayor, engraved with their names.

The clocks were delivered, but my dad never received payment. He billed Jesse a number of times, and Jesse always ignored the bills. At one point, my dad asked Jesse if he could take it out in trade when we'd come into the restaurant. Jesse refused and walked away. My dad swore he would never go to Joe's again, but one time, I came home from college, and that's where I wanted to go for my birthday.

The bill was never paid. And my dad would be turning over in his grave if he knew that Jesse is my father-in-law today.

Jesse knew everyone: Eddie Rickenbacker, Mickey Spillane, Milton Berle, Arthur Godfrey. A few of his off-the-cuff opinions on the famous and infamous:

William Jennings Bryan was a great salesman. He was one of those hellfire types scaring his parishioners. . . . Rumor had it that he was a hell of a chaser, that he chased many a broad around that joint. I liked him. You take them as you find them. He was holier-than-thou, but not really. A lot of it was facade.

I feel sorry for Winchell; he died alone. . . . He came in here two nights before he passed

away. Walter came down in a cab. The cab driver said, what do you do? I was a newspaperman. What's your name? He says, Walter Winchell. The cabdriver says, I never heard of you. He was shocked. I mean, he was shocked.

I knew Meyer for years. I was not an intimate of his, but he was always very gentlemanly. I'm not trying to clean up anything about Meyer Lansky, because I don't know. I've always found him to be a gentleman and that's it.

Some of the best stories about Jesse are from Stephen Sawitz, his grandson. "I was his best pal," Stephen says.

Every time I was with him I'd get butterflies, because it was always exciting. He wanted you to see life and feel life. He would call and say, "Stevie, let's go to lunch." I was four years old. He took me to the airport, we got on an airplane, my first time ever, we flew to Nassau, we had lunch and came back. That was my introduction to flight. He knew I'd like airplanes.

Jesse was a good friend of J. Edgar Hoover and his lifelong companion, Clyde Tolson. Stephen remembers:

Grace Weiss with J. Edgar Hoover and Clyde Tolson.

Manhattan Clam Chowder

At Joe's, this soup is made in 80-gallon steam kettles. Paul Wilson Jr. stirs it with a paddle the size of an oar. His father, who bakes Joe's Key lime pies, used to make it before Paul Jr. was born, but "My son makes the best chowder," he says.

SERVES 8

4 ounces salt pork, cut in ³/₄-inch pieces
2 onions, peeled and chopped coarse
3 medium carrots, chopped
2 ribs celery, trimmed and chopped
2 garlic cloves, minced
1 ¹/₂ pounds chopped clams, with their liquid (see Note)
2 8-ounce bottles clam juice
3 14-ounce cans tomatoes, with liquid

¹/₄ cup tomato paste
¹/₃ cup ketchup
1 tablespoon Maggi seasoning (or Gravy Master or Kitchen Bouquet)
2 teaspoons dried thyme
Salt and pepper
³/₄ pound potatoes, peeled, cut in eighths lengthwise, and sliced
¹/₂ small green pepper, chopped
3 tablespoons flour mixed with 3 tablespoons cold water

Brown the salt pork in a large kettle over low heat, stirring, until golden, about 20 minutes. If there is more than about 2 tablespoons fat, pour off and discard the excess. Add the onions, carrots, and celery and cook over medium-low heat until they begin to soften, about 10 minutes. Add garlic and cook 2 minutes longer.

Drain the clams, reserving their liquid, and set aside. Measure the drained clam liquid; add the bottled clam juice and the liquid from the canned tomatoes. Add enough cold water, if needed, to make a total of 7 cups. Add this liquid and the tomatoes to the vegetables. Stir to break up the tomatoes, then stir in the tomato paste, ketchup, Maggi, thyme, and a pinch of salt and pepper. Simmer, uncovered, for 25 minutes. Add the potatoes and simmer, uncovered, until the potatoes are tender, about 25 minutes longer.

Add the reserved chopped clams and the green pepper to the soup; simmer

5 minutes longer. Stir the flour and cold water mixture into the simmering soup, with a few more grindings of pepper. Simmer 2 minutes longer. Correct seasonings and serve hot.

Note: Either have a fishmonger shuck and chop fresh clams, reserving their liquid, or use frozen or canned chopped clams.

Paul Wilson Jr. and one of the vats of chowder.

*M*ost people get up in the morning and smell coffee and bacon. But at Joe's, we smell chowder and Key lime pie.

—*Paul Wilson Jr.*

Flying back from London, the whole family, when I was a kid. We landed at night, and we were escorted off the plane and the FBI was there. My grandfather would just call up his friend J. Edgar Hoover and arrange to have freedom of the port, so they just got you right through customs. You never knew when he would pull something like that.

Another testimonial to Jesse's closeness to Hoover comes from *Tell It to the King* by Larry King:

Speaking of clout, the first time I went to San Francisco, I was working in Miami and not making a lot of money, just enough to take my first wife for a trip. Jesse Weiss, of Joe's Stone Crab, said to me, "Hey, we'll do it up right. When you land, there'll be a nice surprise for you."

We flew coach to San Francisco, and as we were getting off the plane, a man in a tan overcoat came up to me. I don't know how he knew who I was, but he said, "Mr. King, Mrs. King? Come right with me."

He took us to a limo and introduced himself. "I'm Agent Sanders with the Federal Bureau of Investigation, and I'll be happy to take you anywhere you'd like to go while you're in San Francisco."

Hoover was a great public relations man, it was later explained to me. "You're hosting a

One of my favorite restaurants in America is Joe's Stone Crab in Miami Beach, Florida. The owners, Jesse and Grace Weiss, are dear old friends of mine, and my fame among our chums in Florida is that I am one of a few people who can go in the back way with the fish. Otherwise, it's an hour's wait for a table. A few years ago Miriam and I were enjoying a wonderful meal, and I noticed someone who seemed to recognize me. He looked familiar, but I wasn't sure exactly who he was. I noticed that he and his friend were finishing their meal and were about to light two dinky, cellophane-wrapped, awful-looking cigars. I had three cigars made of the finest Cuban tobacco with me that I had brought back from a recent trip to Europe, where they are legal. I asked the waiter to please give these two cigars to the gentlemen with my compliments. As the waiter left the table, I suddenly realized that I was sending two illegal eight-dollar Havana cigars to J. Edgar Hoover and his friend. And that's all I know about the FBI. Don't ask me for more details!

—*Jack Paar*, P.S. Jack Paar, *1982*

Biscayne and Collins, circa 1930

talk show in Miami," Jesse said, "you're writing a column. How do you think the FBI builds friends around the country?"

But apparently, being Hoover's friend didn't exempt Jesse from J. Edgar's scrutiny. Stephen remembers:

Mr. Hoover invited Jesse to visit his office in the FBI building. Apparently, Hoover had his desk elevated, so he could look down on people. But when Edgar—that's what Jesse called him—left the office, my grandfather went over to his desk—he wanted to see if there was a file on him. And he was in there!

Sometimes, Stephen would find traveling with Jesse unnerving:

We would go to California, for instance, for the Superbowl. Without hotel or car reservations, without Superbowl tickets. We're just going out there blind. I said, "We don't have reservations." He said, "Don't worry, Pete Rozelle left my name at the Fairmont." And he never lost a beat.

He was very unpretentious; he was very disarming like that. One time he said, "Stevie, I want you to meet somebody." And I said okay, and he said, "I want you to meet the next president of the United States," and it was George Bush. And I was like, yeah, right. And what was really touching was that when Bush got into town, the first person he wanted to see was my grandfather. He gave him a bear hug, "Jess, how are ya?!", shook his hand, and I'm thinking, "He's for real. Grandfather's for real." Nothing ceased to amaze me with him.

He would charm twenty-five-year-old women: "I want you to meet my grandson." It was like this mythical aura about him. He loved his cigars, he loved to play cards, he loved jet travel. And he was a good sport, tipping well and treating people very well.

He was also famous for telling customers they were sitting too long—"What do you think this is, a library?"

JESSE WEISS

RITA HAYWORTH AND ORSON WELLES ON VISIT

One of the first local places the couple visited was Joe's Restaurant on Biscayne Street.

—*Miami social column*

Lisa Rosati, manager of Joe's Take Away, remembers

my dad bringing me to Joe's when I was little for my birthday. I loved stone crabs, but it was like forbidden food unless you were in this restaurant. And I remember hearing the stories about Papa, that he doesn't like you holding a table long. So I would eat quickly, you know, "Let's go, let's go, before the man comes." I was intrigued by him but if he came near the table, I panicked. And then all these years later I ended up working here.

Stephen: *How my grandfather got away with all he did, with all his gambling and craziness and everything, I'll never know. On the one hand, he was terrible with money, but then he was also good with people. And somehow he was magic. I thought the sun rose and set on him, and vice versa.*

Allan Myerson: *The man was unique, I tell you.*

Stephen: *He was the best.*

Allan: *He was a pistol.*

Stephen*: Everywhere he went people lit up when they saw him.*

When Jesse Weiss was seventy-five, Miami anchorperson Ann Bishop spent many hours recording his memories. Here's how Jesse concluded the interview:

I want to be remembered as trying to live my life with as little aggravation for others than I have for myself. Unfortunately, I'm a Hungarian, and I'm hot-headed. . . . I think my daughter tells people, don't pay attention to that, and she's smart about it. She's my pride and joy. She's a great mother, she's a great gal, she's got an awful lot of class. She's not money-hungry, she's fast to do for others.

I'm proud of what others have done keeping Joe's going, which I consider a monument to myself. The family all do a hell of a job. I've had a good life.

Now, I want to say one more thing. I'm the most fortunate man in the world, for one reason! My daughter Jo Ann. She has my hot Hungarian temper, but like me, she forgets what she got angry about five minutes after she got angry . . . and I love her dearly. Now, may we close? I've got a barber waiting for me.

Views of Jesse over the years.
BELOW: Jesse welcomes Patricia Neal and friends.

Armand Salad

Armand (pictured opposite) is waiter Armand Bar-Michael, a native of Israel. "I learned this salad at the Canadian Pavilion at Expo '67," Armand says, "where I served Queen Elizabeth and Charles de Gaulle."

Joe's regulars know that this salad is served at lunch only.

SERVES 6 TO 8

Dressing
1 or 2 small garlic cloves
1/4 teaspoon salt
1/2 teaspoon pepper
1 teaspoon mayonnaise
1/4 to 1/3 cup fresh lemon juice
1 teaspoon red wine vinegar
 (optional)
1/4 cup plus 2 tablespoons
 olive oil

1 head romaine lettuce, outer
 leaves removed, washed, dried,
 torn into bite-size pieces
 and chilled

1 small head iceberg lettuce,
 outer leaves removed, washed,
 dried, torn into bite-size pieces,
 and chilled
1/2 cup chopped fresh parsley
1/2 sweet white onion, sliced thin
1/2 cup freshly grated Parmesan
 cheese, plus more for sprinkling
 on top
24 to 32 Garlic Croutons
 (page 79)
Thin slices of green bell pepper,
 for garnish (optional)

Make the dressing in a large salad bowl: Mash the garlic, salt, and pepper to a paste. Add the mayonnaise, continuing to mash until smooth. Then mix in the lemon juice and the vinegar, if using. Gradually add the olive oil, whisking.

Add the lettuces, parsley, onion, and the 1/2 cup Parmesan. Toss gently. Pile the mixture into shallow salad bowls, sprinkle with croutons and a little more Parmesan, and serve.

Joe's head fish cooks are Pedro Morales, who's been at Joe's for forty years, and Eugene "Blue Jay" Green, who's been at Joe's for twenty-two. "These two men are fixtures," says Jo Ann. "They're the work force." Grace remembers when Pedro's father brought him in: "He was a skinny little kid. He started as a dishwasher, and he's a good cook today." Abe Spann has been making salads here for thirty-seven years.

Joe's Vinaigrette Dressing

This is another of Jo Ann's contributions. Salad chefs Abraham Spann (who's been with Joe's for nearly forty years) and Renel Sejour make this dressing in bulk.

MAKES ABOUT 1 3/4 CUPS

1/4 cup chopped onion or scallion
3 tablespoons minced fresh parsley
2 tablepoons chopped pimento
1 chopped hard-cooked egg
2 tablespoons minced chives
1 1/2 teaspoons sugar

1 teaspoon salt
1/2 teaspoon cayenne pepper
1/2 cup drained capers
 (optional)
1/3 cup wine or cider vinegar
3/4 cup olive oil

Whisk together all the ingredients. Store in refrigerator.

Roquefort Dressing

MAKES ABOUT 1 1/3 CUPS

1/2 pound Roquefort, crumbled
3/4 teaspoon Worcestershire
 sauce, or to taste
3/8 teaspoon A-1 sauce, or
 to taste
Pinch of Colman's dry mustard

1/4 cup plus 2 tablespoons light
 cream (or 3 tablespoons each
 heavy cream and milk)
1 1/2 tablespoons cider vinegar
1/2 teaspoon corn or vegetable oil
3/8 teaspoon sugar

Chop or crumble the cheese into small pieces. Place in a mixing bowl and add the Worcestershire, A-1, mustard, 1/4 cup cream, and the vinegar. Mix gently until well combined; then add the oil and sugar. Thin, if necessary, with the remaining cream. Chill until serving.

Garlic Dressing

A thick, creamy dressing. This recipe has been adapted for egg safety.

MAKES 1 CUP

2 eggs
1 tablespoon wine vinegar
$^1\!/_2$ teaspoon salt, or to taste
$^1\!/_2$ teaspoon pepper, or to taste

$^1\!/_2$ teaspoon sugar, or to taste
2 garlic cloves, crushed
1 tablespoon dry mustard
1 cup vegetable oil

Place eggs and vinegar in a glass measuring cup; beat with a fork until smooth. Microwave on high for 1½ minutes, or until eggs are lightly scrambled. Transfer the mixture to a food processor or blender and add the salt, pepper, sugar, garlic, and mustard. Process until well blended.

With the machine running, add the oil a few drops at a time; then in a slow steady stream. Correct all seasonings; chill the dressing until needed.

Garlic Croutons

MAKES 4 CUPS

4 cups $^3\!/_4$-inch cubes cut from
  day-old egg rolls (such as
  challah), or Italian or French
  bread, with crust

3 tablespoons unsalted butter
2 garlic cloves, crushed with
  a knife blade and peeled, but
  left whole

Preheat the oven to 375°F. Place bread cubes in a roasting or jelly roll pan.

Heat the butter and garlic in a small skillet over medium-low heat. Cook, stirring now and then, until the garlic is fragrant and beginning to brown lightly, 3 or 4 minutes. Remove and discard the garlic. Pour the butter over the bread cubes and toss gently to coat well.

Bake, tossing the croutons now and then, until crisp and golden brown, about 5 to 7 minutes. Place the pan on a wire rack to cool; then store the croutons at room temperature, in a plastic bag or airtight container.

Joe's Hash Browns

A Joe's Stone Crab classic. Custom-made crab cooker baskets are used at Joe's to cook four hundred pounds of potatoes at a time; two or three baskets are cooked per night for hash browns. The baskets have ball bearings on the base, so they can be wheeled around the kitchen. The Idaho potatoes are boiled with skins on, drained, refrigerated, then peeled, chopped, and fried. That's a lot of work for hash browns.

At lunch, Paul Wilson Jr. has six to eight seasoned pans of hash browns going at a time; he flips each panful of potatoes with a quick jerk of the wrist. It looks easy, but then he's had twenty years of practice. The method here of inverting the potatoes onto a plate works just as well as Paul's flip.

It's the combination of fat and salt that really makes these. They're for a once-in-a-while splurge, so don't hold back.

SERVES 4

3 medium Idaho potatoes (about 1¼ pounds)

5 tablespoons vegetable oil, or more as needed
Salt and pepper

Peel the potatoes and halve them lengthwise. Cook in boiling salted water until tender but not mushy, 25 to 30 minutes. Drain and cool. Cut the potatoes up roughly, slicing them in thin, irregular pieces. The pieces don't have to be even, but they shouldn't be any larger than a quarter.

Heat 2½ tablespoons of the oil in a 7- or 8-inch nonstick skillet over medium heat. (If you are using a cast iron or other heavy skillet, you may need a little more oil.) When the oil is hot but not smoking, add the potatoes; they should cover the bottom evenly, and the pan should be about ¾ full. (At the restaurant, Paul Jr. scoops up just the right amount of potatoes with an oval plate, then slides them into the pan.) Season the potatoes with salt and pepper. With a wooden spoon or spatula, turn the potatoes over to impregnate them with oil. Gently smooth out the mixture in the pan, pressing it around the edges to form a neat round edge. Sprinkle with a little more salt and pepper, and drizzle with a little more oil.

Let the potatoes cook, without moving them, until you can see that the edges are brown, 10 to 12 minutes. Adjust the heat, if necessary, to maintain a steady, gentle sizzle. Give the pan a little shake now and then to prevent sticking, without disturbing the potatoes. And if needed, add a little more oil in the center of the pan.

When the edges are brown, invert a flat dinner plate over the skillet. Holding the skillet with a pot holder or kitchen towel, invert the potatoes decisively onto the plate. Place the skillet back on the burner, add 2 tablespoons more oil, and carefully slide the potatoes back into the skillet. Sprinkle with a little more salt and pepper.

Let the potatoes sizzle for about 30 seconds. Make a few cuts in the potatoes with the side of the spoon. Cook the second side, adjusting the heat as necessary, until nicely browned, about 10 minutes longer.

Now hold a serving plate over the skillet, and invert the hash browns onto the plate so that the just-browned side is now up. That's it! Serve hot.

VARIATION: LYONNAISE POTATOES

1 small onion, peeled and sliced lengthwise with the grain

1 tablespoon vegetable oil, or as needed

Sauté the onion in the oil over medium heat, tossing occasionally, until lightly golden, about 8 minutes.

Follow the recipe above, but place only about half the potatoes in the pan. Scatter the onions over; then top with the remaining potatoes. Continue to cook as directed above.

BELOW: Paul Wilson Jr. covers the whole stove with pans of hash browns, flipping and frying them to perfection. BELOW RIGHT: The end product—a crispy, golden plateful of Joe's Hash Browns.

Joe's Creamed Spinach

This is one of Jo Ann Bass's contributions to the menu, and it's now a Joe's classic. George Knowles, a cook at Joe's on and off since 1982 (a relative newcomer, though he's been cooking for thirty-eight years), makes this in 80-gallon steam kettles.

SERVES 4

2 10-ounce boxes frozen chopped spinach, thawed
1 ½ cups light cream (or ¾ cup each heavy cream and milk)

1 teaspoon salt
¼ teaspoon nutmeg, or to taste
2 tablespoons unsalted butter
2 tablespoons all-purpose flour

Gently squeeze the spinach, discarding excess water. Place it in a nonaluminum saucepan and cook over low heat, stirring constantly, for 5 minutes, until beginning to become tender, but still bright green.

Add the cream, salt, and nutmeg and simmer for 5 minutes, until the cream has bubbled and reduced slightly.

Meanwhile, melt the butter in a small skillet; add the flour and cook over low heat, stirring, for 3 or 4 minutes, until opaque. Stir this roux into the spinach mixture. Simmer for 4 or 5 minutes longer, until creamy and smooth but still bright green. Correct the seasonings and serve hot.

VARIATION: JOE'S CREAMED GARLIC SPINACH

1 garlic clove, minced

1 teaspoon unsalted butter

Cook the garlic in the butter over medium-low heat until fragrant and softened but not browned, about 3 minutes. Add to the spinach with the roux; then proceed as directed above.

OPPOSITE: Rolando Barriero (left) and Renel Sejour in the kitchen.

COLE SLAW—A JOE'S CLASSIC

Joe's Cole Slaw has been served from the very beginning. It's a recipe of Jennie's, Joe's wife and Jo Ann's grandmother. It starts with very finely shredded cabbage, which is dipped briefly in a vinegar and sugar dressing—Jennie's Hungarian secret recipe. It's then placed in a high mound on a salad plate, like a haystack, and topped with a dollop of mayonnaise, then a spoonful of relish. Two thick tomato slices are propped upright on the sides of the mound. Joe's kitchen goes through over 1,100 pounds of cabbage for each week's supply of cole slaw.

JESSE WEISS

For

years, it was an open Miami Beach secret that you could get Joe's Stone Crabs "to go," if you knocked at the back door. But starting in November 1987, you could get them much more easily—at Joe's Take Away. And there's no dealing with the long lines waiting to get into the restaurant for dinner.

"We built a new section," Jo Ann Bass says, "which houses our Take Away, Stone Crabs, Inc. [the wholesale arm of the business], our own laundry, and more recently, the shipping department."

Jo Ann oversaw the clean look of the operation; Jodi handled most of the details, from menu to layout, equipment, and procedure. Lisa Rosati came in just when the

Take Away was ready to open. Jodi says, "She's good with food, good with people, and upbeat. The three of us—Jodi, Stephen, and Lisa—are excellent working together. We've become like family."

All the popular items from the restaurant menu are available at the Take Away: stone crabs with mustard sauce or melted butter, hash brown potatoes or cottage fried sweets, creamed spinach, cole slaw, Key lime and apple pies. "Very clean, very simple food," Lisa says. The Take Away also sells its own specialties: Jodi's grilled chicken and fish sandwiches (big sellers); conch seviche; pasta, potato, and taboulleh salads; outstanding bread pudding. At lunchtime, customers are often from the film crews and photo shoots that now abound on South Beach. At dinner, they do a brisk business with customers who want to enjoy Joe's food at home.

"In December of 1987," Lisa remembers, "*USA Today* called us; they included us in a Christmas story on mail-order foods. Up until then, we had little cooler boxes in which we'd pack crabs for people to take on an airplane; and once or twice a week, we'd ship crabs with Federal Express. After that article, our shipping business took off, and it hasn't stopped since."

Last New Year's Eve, the Take Away did $35,000 in sales on one day—and that was just walk-in business, without shipping.

After having custom boxes designed (emblazoned with a big red crab, naturally), the shipping business recently expanded. Orders now come in from all over the country—from regular customers, from people who have heard of but never been to Joe's Stone Crab, from such celebrities as Quincy Jones, Ann-Margret, and Senator Ted Kennedy. One day, taking an order on the phone, Lisa was trying to reassure a customer. "Will we get by your security? I've sent crabs to the president at the White House. They got by their bomb detectors, so I know they'll get to you. . . . Great, we'll be happy to."

"Who was that?" a visitor asked.

"It's Frank Sinatra's birthday," Lisa said, "and we're sending him stone crabs in Las Vegas."

PREVIOUS PAGES: The look of Joe's Stone Crab Restaurant hasn't changed much over the years, though dining rooms and the Take Away business have been added. RIGHT: The restaurant was declared a Miami Beach hallmark in 1975.

JOE'S TAKE AWAY

Jodi's Grilled Chicken Sandwich

MAKES 2 SANDWICHES

2 5- to 6-ounce boneless,
  skinless chicken breast halves,
  fat and tendons trimmed
½ cup bottled Italian dressing
2 sesame or other rolls, split

2 romaine lettuce leaves
2 slices of ripe tomato
1 thin slice of onion, separated
  into rings

Pound the chicken breast halves between two sheets of wax paper or plastic wrap to a thickness of ½ inch. Place the dressing in a shallow soup bowl; dip in the chicken. (If you have time, the chicken can marinate in the dressing, covered and refrigerated, for ½ to 1 hour.)

Preheat a grill or a skillet, preferably nonstick, over medium heat. Lift the chicken from the dressing, letting excess drip off. Cook the chicken until lightly golden, about 2 minutes per side. (Lower the heat slightly if necessary; the chicken should sizzle gently.) Place each breast half on the bottom half of a roll. Top with lettuce, tomato, and a few pieces of onion. Cover with the tops of the rolls and serve.

President Truman and his party enjoyed a stone crab dinner during their Key West visit, because, through "Weiss" channels, Jesse Weiss, owner of Joe's Stone Crab restaurant, iced up 50 pounds of the claws of the famous delicacy, propagated in the Florida Keys, and sent them by air express to the chief executive. Vice-President-Elect Nixon said he attended an informal dinner party last night as the guest of Gov. Thomas E. Dewey of New York at Joe's Stone Crab.

—Miami Daily News, *November 20, 1952*

Jodi's Grilled Grouper Sandwich

MAKES 2 SANDWICHES

2 4-ounce grouper (or other
  fish) fillets
½ cup bottled Italian dressing
2 sesame or other rolls, split
2 romaine lettuce leaves

2 slices of ripe tomato
1 thin slice of onion, separated
  into rings
Tartar sauce

    Place the dressing in a shallow soup bowl; dip in the fish. (If you have time, the fish can marinate in the dressing, refrigerated, for ½ to 1 hour.)

    Preheat a grill or a skillet, preferably nonstick, over medium to medium-low heat. Lift the fish from the dressing, letting excess drip off. Cook the fish until opaque and lightly golden, 3 or 4 minutes per side. Place each fillet on the bottom half of a roll. Top with lettuce, tomato, and a few pieces of onion. Cover with the tops of the rolls and serve, with tartar sauce on the side.

A wholesale price list at the fishery.

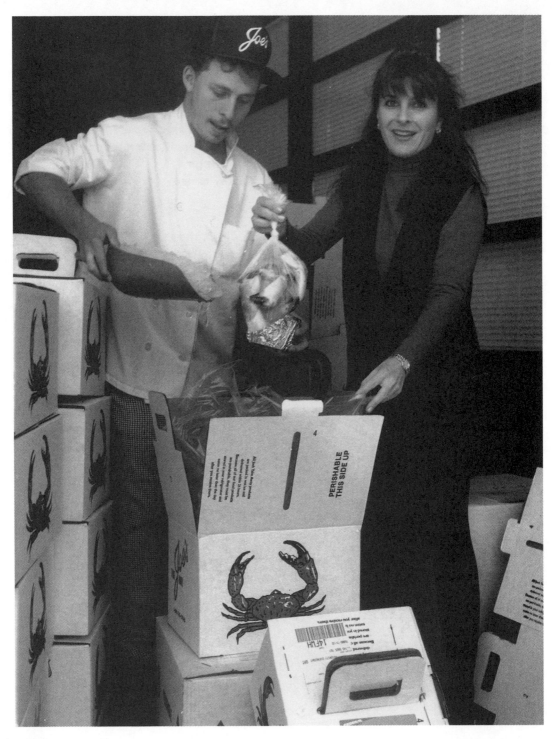

New Potato Salad

SERVES ABOUT 8

3 pounds small red new
  potatoes, scrubbed
Salt
¾ cup mayonnaise
¾ cup sour cream or plain
  low-fat yogurt

¾ teaspoon pepper, or to taste
1 small to medium red onion,
  peeled, halved, and sliced thin
¼ cup chopped fresh dill
¼ cup chopped fresh parsley,
  preferably flat-leaf

Place the potatoes in a saucepan; add cold water to cover by about 1 inch. Bring to a boil; add salt. Boil gently until the potatoes are tender but not mushy, usually 15 to 20 minutes. Drain the potatoes in a colander.

Meanwhile, in a large measuring cup, stir together the mayonnaise, sour cream, 1 to 1½ teaspoons salt, and pepper.

When the potatoes are cool enough to handle but still warm, cut them in quarters (or eighths, if potatoes are larger), leaving the skins on. Drop them into a large mixing bowl. Add the onion, dill, parsley, and the mayonnaise mixture. Toss gently, without breaking up the potatoes. Serve at room temperature or slightly chilled.

Following their week's cruise in these waters aboard Jock Whitney's yacht, Jock and his guest CBS's Bill Paley stopped off here just for the specialty of the house at Joe's Stone Crabs.

—George Bourke, "Night Life," Miami Herald

Rank hath its privileges. When we went down to Key Biscayne with Nixon, Joe's was the only redemption as far as I'm concerned.

—John Erlichman

OPPOSITE: John Masur helps Take Away manager Lisa Rosati pack stone crabs for shipping.

Tortellini Salad

SERVES 4 TO 6

1 pound cheese tortellini, preferably tricolor
1 large ripe tomato (or 2 plum tomatoes), cored, seeded, and cut into ¼-inch dice
½ small green bell pepper, trimmed and cut into ¼-inch dice
4 scallions, trimmed and sliced
1 or 2 garlic cloves, crushed
½ cup plus 2 tablespoons olive oil
2 tablespoons balsamic vinegar, or to taste

2 tablespoons chopped fresh parsley
½ teaspoon Lawry's seasoned salt (optional)
¾ teaspoon dried basil
Pinch of lemon pepper seasoning (optional)
Salt and pepper
1 teaspoon chopped fresh cilantro (optional)
½ teaspoon Italian seasoning (or use a blend of dried marjoram, thyme, rosemary, and oregano)

Cook the tortellini, uncovered, in a large pot of boiling salted water until just tender but not mushy, about 12 minutes.

Meanwhile, place the tomato, bell pepper, scallions, and garlic in a large mixing bowl. Add the oil, vinegar, parsley, and seasonings, stirring gently to blend. Drain the pasta well; add it to the mixing bowl and toss gently. Correct seasonings; cool and chill before serving.

Transcripts of bugged calls in the Watergate conspiracy mentioned Joe's Stone Crabs. E. Howard Hunt, who was convicted for his part in Watergate, had in his list of private telephone numbers a number not listed in the telephone directory which rings at the Miami Beach restaurant. Jesse Weiss, operator of Joe's Stone Crabs, said in an interview . . . that he did not know Hunt "and I wouldn't know him if I fell over him. He probably called for reservations." He said, however, that former White House top aides John Erlichman and H. R. Haldeman, along with presidential press secretary Ronald Ziegler, dine at the restaurant frequently when President Nixon visits Key Biscayne. Weiss said that if Hunt called for reservations, "We probably told him we don't take reservations."

—Miami News, *June 5, 1973*

ucumber Salad

Don't use waxed cukes for this dish.

SERVES 4

2 pounds (3 or 4) cucumbers, unpeeled and sliced thin	**¹/₂ cup cider vinegar**
1 ¹/₂ teaspoons salt	**³/₄ cup sugar**
	1 red onion, sliced thin

Place the cucumber slices in a colander and sprinkle with the salt. Set aside to drain for ¹/₂ hour.

Gently squeeze the cucumbers dry and transfer to a glass serving dish; stir in the vinegar, sugar, and onion. Cover and chill at least 1 hour. Correct seasonings if necessary.

Top chefs no average Joes when dining out

By GEOFFREY TOMB
Herald Staff Writer

They are titans in toque, kings of kitchendom, all Gaul divided into six parts, half-dozen of the greatest living chefs of France, exported to Miami to cook din for 65. Together. In one place. Tonight.

But first a little something to eat. A simple little place on Miami Beach called Joe's.

So what do famous French chefs eat when dining out? No quail eggs or lamb's brains or puppy dog tails.

For one table Friday night there were 15 plates of large stone crabs, five claws to a plate at $22.50 per plate plus sweet potato cottage fries, hash browns, a few steaks, house salad and Key lime pie.

"*C'est bon,*" said chef Michel Lorain, slightly timid in dealing with his very first huge stone crab.

Unlike most weekend patrons of the restaurant, the chefs did not have to wait in line.

"A professional courtesy," said owner Steve Sawitz.

The six are Paul Bocuse, Gaston Lenotre, Lorain, Jacques Maximin, Pierre Troisgros and Michel Rostang, who missed the restaurant dinner because he was flying in from Los Angeles rather than Paris.

They are here to pay off a debt for charity. Last January, the services of the six, including food and wines, were auctioned at a fund-raiser in Paris for Very Special Arts, a program of the Kennedy Foundation that helps handicapped children

BRUUN OVER MIAMI
by PAUL M. BRUUN

POTPOURRI: Helen Traubel the star at the Fontainebleau Hotel, just received word that she has won the Look Magazine award the best newcomer to the motion picture making colony, for her ... in "Deep In My Heart." The award will be presented to her her first show in the La Ronde Room, next Tuesday night . . . . Matas, vocalist-singer, bows into Jerry Brooks Patio tonight . . . op Berle's in-laws, Mr. and Mrs. Michael Rosenthal, are winte at the South Seas Hotel . . . The Charlie Mastico Trio opens

ABOVE: Paul Bruun announces the arrival of Jodi, Jo Ann and "Say's" first child. LEFT: French chefs Paul Bocuse and Jacques Maximin clown around.

Taboulleh Salad

SERVES 8 TO 10

1 cup bulgur (steamed cracked wheat)
3/4 cup boiling water
3 medium cucumbers, peeled, seeded, and diced
1 1/2 cups chopped red onion
1 cup chopped celery
3/4 cup diced green bell pepper
1/2 cup coarsely chopped ripe black olives (about 18 medium)
3/4 cup plus 2 tablespoons olive oil
1/4 cup red wine vinegar
2 tablespoons lemon juice

1/2 cup chopped fresh parsley
1/4 cup chopped fresh mint, or 2 tablespoons dried
3 tablespoons chopped fresh basil leaves, or 1/2 teaspoon dried
1/4 teaspoon dried oregano
Salt and pepper
2 pounds ripe tomatoes (regular or plum), cored, halved, seeded, and cut into 1/2 -inch dice
1 pound feta cheese, rinsed and crumbled into 1/2 -inch pieces
Salad greens, for garnish

Stir together the bulgur and boiling water in a large mixing bowl. Set aside until lukewarm.

Add the cucumber, onion, celery, bell pepper, olives, olive oil, vinegar, lemon juice, parsley, mint, basil, oregano, and salt and pepper. Stir everything together gently until combined. Cover and chill the mixture.

Gently stir the tomatoes into the tabouleh; then add the feta cheese and combine gently, without breaking up the cheese too much. Add more salt and pepper to taste. Line a platter or bowl with salad greens; spoon the tabouleh over the greens and serve cool.

At Joe's Stone Crab emporium Dorothy Lamour munches the famed delicacy for lunch before entraining out for New York.

—*Miami social column*

William Powell . . . and his pretty young wife . . . enjoyed you-know-what last night at Joe's Stone Crabs.

—The Evening Sun, *November 5, 1946*

French-Fried Zucchini with Horseradish Sauce

SERVES 6

4 medium zucchini
3 eggs
3 tablespoons cold water
¾ teaspoon salt
1 cup all-purpose flour
1¾ cups seasoned dry bread
 crumbs, or as needed

3 tablespoons chopped fresh
 parsley
4 cups vegetable oil, or as needed
 for deep-frying
Horseradish Sauce (recipe follows)
Lemon wedges

Slice the zucchini, leaving the skin on, into rounds slightly less than ¼-inch thick.

Set up breading: In a shallow bowl, beat the egg with the water and salt. Next to this, place the flour in a pie plate or shallow bowl. Alongside, combine the bread crumbs and parsley in a third pie plate or shallow bowl.

Dip the zucchini slices into the egg mixture. Lift them out with a skimmer, draining off excess, and dip them into the flour. Lift them out, shaking off excess, and dip them back into the egg wash. Now dip them into the bread crumbs, coating them well. Lift them out, shaking off excess crumbs, and place on a wax paper–lined baking sheet. Refrigerate for at least ½ hour.

Heat the oil in a deep skillet or casserole to a temperature of 350 to 360°F. When the oil reaches 350°F, a pinch of flour will sizzle energetically as it hits the oil; a cube of bread will turn golden in about 30 seconds. Adjust the heat to maintain a steady temperature. Fry the zucchini slices until golden brown, turning them once, 2 to 3 minutes. Drain well and keep warm while you fry the remaining zucchini. Serve hot, with Horseradish Sauce or lemon.

HORSERADISH SAUCE

⅔ cup mayonnaise
3 tablespoons drained bottled
 white horseradish

1 teaspoon fresh lemon
 juice

Stir the ingredients together. Cover and refrigerate until serving.

Bread Pudding

SERVES ABOUT 8

3 cups ³/₄-inch bread cubes,
  preferably day-old challah
  (or French or Italian bread)
2 tablespoons unsalted butter,
  melted
¹/₂ cup raisins, soaked in warm
  water if very dry
³/₄ cup sugar
¹/₂ teaspoon cinnamon
¹/₂ teaspoon nutmeg

6 eggs
2 egg yolks
6 cups milk
1 tablespoon plus 1 teaspoon
  pure vanilla extract

Topping
¹/₃ cup sugar
³/₄ teaspoon cinnamon
³/₄ teaspoon nutmeg

Preheat the oven to 350°F. Place the bread cubes in a 9-inch square baking pan; toss with the melted butter. Drain the raisins well, discarding the liquid; add the raisins to the bread and toss gently.

In a large mixing bowl, whisk the sugar, cinnamon, and nutmeg until combined. Add the eggs and egg yolks, whisking until smooth. Add the milk and vanilla and whisk until well combined.

Combine the sugar, cinnamon, and nutmeg for the topping, and set aside. Place the baking pan in a larger roasting pan. Pour most of the egg mixture over the bread. Place the roasting pan on the center oven rack; carefully pour in the remaining egg mixture. Sprinkle the topping mixture over the surface. Pour enough hot water into the larger pan to come about halfway up the pudding.

Bake until lightly golden and just set, but still slightly wobbly in the center, about 1 to 1¼ hours (timing can vary; do not overbake). Carefully remove the pudding from the water bath and cool on a wire rack. When cool, refrigerate. Serve cold or at room temperature.

Aside to Jack "H-T" Pepper: Your exultation over those stone crabs at Joe's down at the South End of the beach was merely the echo of numerous other greats, to wit: presidents Roosevelt, Harding and Coolidge, Charles A. Lindbergh, Joe E. Lewis, etc.

—Miami social column

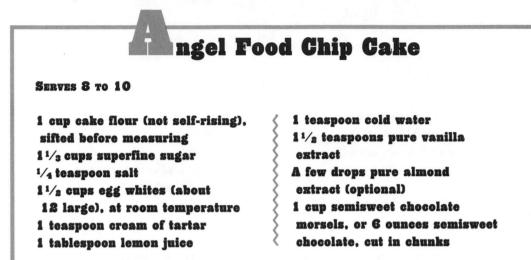

Angel Food Chip Cake

SERVES 8 TO 10

1 cup cake flour (not self-rising),
 sifted before measuring
1 ⅓ cups superfine sugar
¼ teaspoon salt
1 ½ cups egg whites (about
 12 large), at room temperature
1 teaspoon cream of tartar
1 tablespoon lemon juice

1 teaspoon cold water
1 ½ teaspoons pure vanilla
 extract
A few drops pure almond
 extract (optional)
1 cup semisweet chocolate
 morsels, or 6 ounces semisweet
 chocolate, cut in chunks

Preheat the oven to 350°F. Cut a sheet of parchment or wax paper to fit the bottom of a 10-inch tube pan, preferably one with a removable bottom. Fit paper in pan; set aside.

Sift the flour, ⅓ cup of the sugar, and the salt onto a sheet of wax paper. Sift this mixture three more times, working back and forth between two sheets of wax paper; set flour mixture aside. Sift remaining 1 cup sugar onto another sheet of wax paper; set aside.

Beat egg whites with an electric mixer at medium-low speed until foamy. Add the cream of tartar, lemon juice, water, vanilla, and, if using, almond extract; increase speed to slightly higher than medium and beat until the whites are nearly stiff. Lower mixer speed and add the cup of sifted sugar to the whites, 2 tablespoons at a time. Continue to beat until peaks are stiff but not dry.

Sift about ¼ of the flour mixture onto the egg whites; fold in gently with a large rubber spatula. Repeat three times; then gently fold in the chocolate morsels. Gently pour the batter into the prepared pan. Run a knife through the mixture to eliminate air pockets; smooth the top with a spatula.

Bake until the top of the cake is lightly golden and the cake springs back when pressed lightly, about 45 minutes. Remove cake from oven and invert it, still in pan, either on the pan's supporting "legs" or over the narrow neck of a bottle. Let the cake hang until cooled completely.

Run a thin, sharp knife blade around inside edges of cooled cake pan; unmold cake. Cut wedges of cake with a serrated knife or cake "comb" and serve with Light Chocolate Mousse (see page 100).

An Angel Food Chip Cake
cools after baking.

ight Chocolate Mousse

Serve this with Angel Food Chip Cake.

MAKES 3 TO 4 CUPS

2 cups heavy or whipping cream, well chilled
3 tablespoons unsweetened cocoa powder

3 tablespoons confectioners' sugar
2 teaspoons pure vanilla extract

   With an electric mixer or wire whisk, whip the cream until it starts to become fluffy.

   Add the cocoa, confectioners' sugar, and vanilla and whip until the cream forms soft peaks. Do not overwhip. If not serving immediately, chill.

Everyone at Joe's calls the black-and-white tile motif "Chiclets."

Coconut Chip Blondies

This recipe can be doubled and baked in a 10½ x 15½-inch jelly roll pan.

MAKES 1 DOZEN

½ cup chopped pecans
½ cup unsalted butter, softened
⅓ cup granulated sugar
⅓ cup brown sugar
1 egg
1 teaspoon pure vanilla extract

1 cup plus 2 tablespoons flour
½ teaspoon baking soda
¼ teaspoon salt
1 cup semisweet chocolate morsels
1¼ cups shredded coconut

Preheat the oven to 350°F. Butter a 9-inch square baking pan; set aside. Place the pecans in a pie plate or shallow baking pan; place in the oven until the nuts are fragrant, 8 to 10 minutes. Set aside.

In the bowl of an electric mixer, cream the butter with the sugars at medium speed until light. Add the egg, then the vanilla, mixing until blended.

Sift the flour with the baking soda and salt onto a sheet of wax paper. Lower the mixer speed and add the flour, mixing just until blended, no longer. Add the chocolate morsels, coconut, and pecans and mix just until evenly distributed. Transfer the dough to the baking pan, spreading it evenly.

Bake for 20 minutes, or until the top is dry and golden brown and a toothpick inserted into the center of the mixture comes out nearly clean. Cool the pan on a wire rack, then cut into twelve 2 x 3-inch bars.

Two famed television Senatorial investigating personalities just missed meeting last week at Joe's Stone Crab restaurant—Sen. Estes Kefauver and Roy Cohn.

—*Hy Gardner*, New York Herald Tribune, *November 22, 1955*

Bing Crosby will dine on stone crabs from Joe's of Miami Beach tonight—but he'll be 3,000 miles away from the beach. The stone crabs winged west Friday afternoon.

—*George Bourke*, Miami Herald, *December 11, 1954*

The Joe's Family

Again

and again, Joe's owners and employees credit the restaurant's success to its family solidarity. They're referring not only to the Weiss family, of which Jo Ann is the third generation, and her children, Stephen and Jodi, the fourth, but also to the extended family of Joe's employees, many of whom have been with Joe's for as long as forty years. Some have even seen their children enter and stay with Joe's.

"It's been a very loving family for all of us, and for the Miami community, too," says Jodi. The restaurant and its employees support Better Way, a halfway house for the homeless, helped with Hurricane Andrew relief, and much more. "I've never seen anyone hungry turned away at our back door, either," Stephen says. "That will never happen in my lifetime.

MIAMI BEACH
march 1938

"Being fourth-generation," he adds, "you have big shoes to fill, on the one hand, and then you have your own. My mom, my dad, my grandparents, had different styles of management, and I think the situation here now is we're much more of a horizontal company. Mom is at the top, and everybody else in managerial is right below that."

"If I was able to maintain any sense of security in life," says Jo Ann Bass, "I owe it to my father—whose love was *always* unconditional—and to a big old fortress of a building called Joe's—where I grew up and which was filled with people who nurtured me with love and support. As a child, I thought Joe's would always be there (a friend once called Joe's my Tara); as an adult, I strive to make that possible."

PREVIOUS PAGES: At the family table: Stephen Sawitz, Lori Kahn, Matthew Johnson, Jodi Koganovsky; INSET (top row): Tara Murphy, Jeff Bass, Stephen Sawitz, Bob Bass, Jo Ann Bass, Ira Koganovsky, Jodi Koganovsky, Lisa Rosati; (bottom row): Bob Bass Jr., Cindy Bass, Lauren Hershey, Jessica Hershey. ABOVE: Jo Ann Bass as a young girl, in Joe's courtyard. RIGHT: Grace Weiss.

Rose ("Aunt Rose"), Jo Ann's closest friend—"since the day we met in 1955"—helps her oversee just about every aspect of the business. She and her husband, Dick McDaniel, chief seafood inspector, have been at Jo Ann's side for thirty and twenty years, respectively. (Both are also expert horologists, with years of expertise in antique clocks.) "The things Jo Ann does for other people," Rose says, "much of it will never be known."

This kind of closeness has been nurtured for generations. Grace Weiss, who ran Joe's for years with Jesse, remembers two of Joe's chefs, Rabbi and Seabreeze (everyone at Joe's has a nickname). Both now deceased, they were with Joe's for fifty years.

Grace: They had started with Jesse's father as dishwashers. And when they retired, Rabbi and Seabreeze taught the young men to cook. And these are the men who are still cooking here now. And a lot of them are family, because they bring in their sons. We've always done that. It's like an on-the-job training program.

Jo Ann: Their real names were Horatio Johnson and Benson Gardner. Horatio would mimic my grandmother speaking Yiddish, so they called him Rabbi. Seabreeze got his nickname because my grandfather came along once when Benson was sleeping. And he said to him, "What are you doing?" And Benson said, "I'm feeling the sea breeze." And my grandfather said, "Well, Seabreeze, you want a job?" And Benson said, "Yes, sir." And that's how he came to be Seabreeze.

Grace: He was with us all his life. They did a story on those two in Reader's Digest.

The staff eats a good lunch and dinner together every day. And every night, before Joe's opens for dinner at five o'clock, the key players gather for dinner at the "family table." The group might include Jo Ann, Stephen, Jodi, manager Bob Moorehead, chief financial officer Allan Myerson, Rose and Dick McDaniel, and Take Away manager Lisa Rosati. They sit, eating and bantering, while they are served by Eddie Rolle, a waiter with seventeen years of experience, regal bearing, and the world's happiest smile.

Bob Moorehead was a policeman for twenty-seven years. "For twenty of those years," he says, "I worked right out front of Joe's. Then Jo Ann asked me to come to work, and now I'm general manager. A few years back, a hotel developer tried to hire me away to run a competing crab restaurant. 'Why are you holding out?' he asked me; 'it's not as if you're family.' 'These people *are* my family,' I told him."

Calvin Keel, the kitchen manager, came to work at Joe's at the age of nineteen, starting out as a busboy. Today, he does all of the buying (except seafood) and has hired "everybody that's here except three that were here when I got here." Recently, Jo Ann Bass had this to say about him:

Calvin Keel was valedictorian of his senior high school class and was hoping to go on to medical school. Unfortunately, because of a domestic situation, he was unable to further his education. Cal has become one of the key people to the success of our business. He is not only our kitchen manager, but also works as a dining room manager, working in a liaison capacity with our customers.

ABOVE (clockwise from left): Dick McDaniel, Bobby Moorehead, Calvin Keel, and Allan Myerson.

"We've been together for over thirty years," Jo Ann says. "He is my right hand, and I could not operate Joe's without him."

Calvin says, "Everybody here tries to help each other out. This is my life right here." In March 1992, Calvin represented Joe's at a March of Dimes gourmet gala in Washington, D.C. It was his first time to Washington, and he stayed at the home of Senator Bob Graham.

"You really can't understand the great feeling of love and kindness that the family of Joe's has for all of the employees," Calvin says, "unless you are one of the lucky ones who work there."

Allan Myerson is the former owner of the Breakwater Hotel. After selling the hotel, "I told myself I was going to take six months off and play golf. So I played golf every day for a week—and I was pulling my hair out. I told them at Joe's, 'Look, I'll bring your work up to date.' Well, I'm still here."

Rose McDaniel: We do what other places do, we try to buy the best food. But it's just the people—this is a people restaurant. From the customers to the back door, to the managers. We've got over seventy waiters, over two hundred on the payroll. Everybody cares about Joe's.

Lisa Rosati: You've got to be there. That's what makes the Take Away work, too. We're connected.

Allan Myerson: This is like a community unto itself.

Roy Garret, Joe's legendary maître d': *Nobody treats the help like this family does. It's an unbelievable family.*

Grace Weiss: *Joe's has always been a family. Because even today, and Jo Ann still does it, if someone doesn't show up, or there was a need—we weren't calling from the yacht or from the country club. We were always there. And if you had to go in the kitchen and make salads, or run the dishwasher late at night, or whatever, you went in and did it. And that includes Rose and Jodi—everybody. Because we've always been a working family.*

The recipes in this chapter are all family favorites.

BELOW: John La Pocta (right) puts the finishing touches on his tray.

THE WAITERS

Joe's has a waitstaff of more than seventy, many of whom have been with the restaurant for decades. The waiters, both men and women, wear tuxedos (they call themselves "penguins"), often with brightly colored bow ties, adorned with a gold pin in the shape of a whole crab. In the employee training manual, the waiters are reminded that "You work for the best restaurant in the world!"

THE JOE'S FAMILY

Camarones Seviche

Jo Ann Bass tasted this chilled marinated shrimp soup in Peru, where it is served with crunchy popped corn kernels on the side. This is her adaptation; it's delicious and refreshing in warm weather.

SERVES 6

2 pounds medium shrimp
1 cup fresh lime juice
1/4 onion, sliced
1 1/4 cups fresh orange juice
1 cup cored, seeded, and coarsely pureed ripe tomatoes
1 tablespoon prepared salsa
2 jalapeño peppers, seeded and minced
1/2 teaspoon Maggi seasoning (or Gravy Master or Kitchen Bouquet)

2 teaspoons Worcestershire sauce
1 tablespoon Pickapeppa sauce (if available)
2 1/2 tablespoons brown sugar
1/4 cup ketchup
1 teaspoon salt
1/4 teaspoon pepper
Dash of Tabasco sauce
1 ripe tomato, cored and cut in small dice, for garnish
Thin lime slices, for garnish

Bring a saucepan of water to a boil. Add salt and drop in the shrimp. Cook the shrimp just until they turn pink, about 1 to 3 minutes. Drain well. Shell and devein the shrimp; place in a nonaluminum container with the lime juice and onion. Cool; then cover and chill for 1 hour.

Stir in all remaining ingredients except tomato and lime garnishes and chill several hours or overnight. Correct seasonings and serve cold, garnished with diced tomato and lime slices.

I think the real secret of success is the fact that while things here have changed for the better, Joe's doesn't really change. People can come years later and they enjoy themselves here.

—*Roy Garret, maître d'*

eviche

At Joe's, this colorful seviche is made with conch, which is native to the Florida Keys. It works equally well with sea or bay scallops.

SERVES 4 TO 6

1 1/4 pounds conch or scallops, cut in 1/2-inch pieces
1 cup fresh lime juice
1 medium red onion, diced
2 red or green bell peppers, trimmed, and cut in 1/4-inch dice

2 tomatoes, cored, seeded, and cut in 1/4-inch dice
6 pepperoncini peppers (available in jars), seeded and diced
2 tablespoons pepperoncini liquid
5 dashes Tabasco sauce, or to taste

Combine the conch or scallops with the lime juice in a nonmetal bowl. Cover and refrigerate for 3 hours or overnight.

Drain the conch, discarding the lime juice. Combine the seafood with the onion, peppers, tomatoes, pepperoncini and liquid, and Tabasco. Mix well. Refrigerate and serve chilled.

Dijon Shrimp

Jo Ann often serves these at home, with drinks.

SERVES 6 TO 8 AS AN APPETIZER

1 lime
1 1/2 to 2 pounds shrimp

Dijon Dressing
1/4 cup Dijon mustard
1/4 cup red or white wine vinegar
1/4 cup tarragon vinegar
1/4 cup minced shallots
1/4 cup chopped fresh parsley

1/2 teaspoon dried red pepper
 flakes, or to taste
1 or 2 garlic cloves, minced
1 teaspoon salt
Pepper
1/2 cup olive oil

Lime or lemon wedges,
 for garnish

Bring a saucepan of salted water to a boil. Cut the lime in half, squeeze the juice into the water, and drop in the lime halves. Cook the shrimp just until they turn pink, usually about 3 minutes.

For the Dijon Dressing: While the water is coming to a boil, place the mustard, vinegars, shallots, parsley, pepper flakes, garlic, and salt and pepper in a mixing bowl. Whisk until blended; then gradually whisk in the olive oil.

When the shrimp are cooked, drain them well; then peel and devein them. Add them to the dressing while still warm; toss gently and cool. Chill for several hours or overnight; then correct seasonings and serve in a bowl, garnished with lime or lemon wedges.

James T. Jones ("J.T." or "Bones"), now a front-door captain, who has been at Joe's for twenty-three years: "It's the only job I know," he says in a resonant bass, "and the only job I want. We all came up together. I was head busman here for eleven years. Two years ago, I went out on the floor. I raised two kids here; my daughter is in college. I've had my ups and down here, but I wouldn't trade this job for anything."

OPPOSITE: James T. Jones

Blueberry Kuchen

This is a recipe Jo Ann has made for years. It has a nice, buttery cookie crust. Halved seedless red grapes can be substituted for the blueberries.

SERVES 8

Dough
1 ½ cups all-purpose flour
3 tablespoons granulated sugar
Salt
¾ cup unsalted butter, softened
1 tablespoon white vinegar

Filling
4 cups blueberries, rinsed, picked
  over, and shaken dry
1 cup granulated sugar
2 tablespoons all-purpose flour
Pinch of cinnamon

Confectioners' sugar,
  for sprinkling

For the dough: Preheat the oven to 350°F. Butter a 9-inch springform pan; set aside. In a food processor or mixing bowl, combine the flour, sugar, and a pinch of salt. Add the butter and either pulse in the processor or rub into the dry ingredients until the mixture is crumbly. Sprinkle on the vinegar and combine just until the mixture begins to clump together, adding a few drops of water if necessary. With lightly floured fingertips, press the dough into the bottom of the pan. Push the dough 1 inch up the sides of the pan, forming a neat edge.

For the filling: Set aside 1 cup of the blueberries. Toss the remaining 3 cups blueberries in a mixing bowl with the sugar, flour, and cinnamon. Pour into the crust. Bake for about 1 hour, until the crust is golden.

Remove from oven. Scatter the remaining cup of raw blueberries on top. Cool on a wire rack. Refrigerate the cake for at least 1 hour. Carefully run a knife blade around the sides of the pan; unlock and remove the sides. Let stand at room temperature for about 15 minutes before serving, sprinkled with confectioners' sugar.

Chocolate Crispies

This is a wonderful cookie—it has the flavor of a brownie, but is thin and crunchy.

MAKES 2 DOZEN COOKIES

1 ounce unsweetened chocolate, chopped
¼ cup unsalted butter, cut into pieces
½ cup sugar
1 egg, unbeaten

¼ cup sifted all-purpose flour
Salt
¼ teaspoon pure vanilla extract
¼ cup walnuts or pecans, chopped fine

Preheat the oven to 400°F. Generously butter two 8-inch-square baking pans, or one 9 x 13-inch pan; set aside. Melt the chocolate and butter in a double boiler over hot water. Remove from heat.

Add the sugar, egg, flour, pinch of salt, and vanilla to the chocolate mixture and beat until well combined.

Spread the mixture in a very thin, even layer in the pan(s). Bake 13 to 15 minutes, until lightly browned around the edges. Watch carefully to be sure the edges don't get too dark. The cookies will still be slightly soft in the middle.

While still warm, cut the cookies to make 2-inch squares. When cool, break along cut edges into squares.

Moses "Mo" Battle, at Joe's for seventeen years, and Nat Allen, for twenty-seven years, moved up from busmen to waiters. Says Mo: "I'm very happy here. Very happy. No complaints whatsoever."

I'm still here, I love it. This is different from other restaurants—the people you work for, the colleagues. This is my adopted family.

—Bernhard Lukoschek, waiter, twenty-five years

7

9

11

Some of the Joe's family: (1) Rose McDaniel, (2) parking attendants, (3) Eugene "Bluejay" Green, (4) Andrew Rubin and Charles Geslicki, (5) "Say," Steve, and Jodi, (6) Gideon Dareus, (7) Arnold Price, (8) William Jones, (9) James Augostino, (10) Legendary maitre d' Roy Garret, (11) Nat Allan and Lloyd Godwin.

Corn Melba

This is one of Jo Ann's favorites, which she learned from cookbook author Maida Heatter (the "Queen of Desserts"), who graciously allowed us to print an adaptation of her recipe. These are unique paper-thin crackers, crisp and irresistible. Try them with soup or with a glass of wine.

MAKES ABOUT 80 CRACKERS

1/2 cup unsalted butter, softened	2 cups sifted all-purpose flour
2 tablespoons sugar	2 teaspoons baking powder
1/4 teaspoon salt, plus more as needed	1 cup milk
	1 cup water
2 eggs	1/2 cup cornmeal

Preheat the oven to 375°F, with two racks near the center level. Butter two 10½ by 15½-inch jelly roll pans (you can use pans of any size, as long as you keep the batter very thin).

In the bowl of an electric mixer, mix the butter, sugar, and salt until well combined. Add the eggs one at a time. Meanwhile, resift the flour with the baking powder. Lower the mixer speed and add the flour to the butter mixture alternately with the milk and water, beginning and ending with flour. Add the cornmeal and mix just until blended. If there are lumps in the batter, strain it.

Pour ¾ cup plus 2 tablespoons of batter into each pan, tilting the pans to spread the batter as thin as possible. Try to make sure the edges aren't too thin. (It's easier to spread the batter when the pans are warm; heat them briefly in the oven if you like.) Sprinkle the surface of the batter lightly with salt. Bake for 8 minutes, exchanging the rack positions of the pans halfway through. With a sharp knife, cut the batter in each pan into 16 squares.

Return the pans to the oven and continue to bake until the crackers are crisp and medium gold. This usually takes about 5 minutes for the crackers near the edges, about 10 minutes for the ones in the center. With a wide spatula, transfer the browned crackers to a wire rack; continue baking the remaining crackers until they are all evenly colored. (To brown them evenly, it's a good idea to turn the browned edges from the outside of the pan toward the center, and the pale edges from the center toward the outside.) Transfer the baked crackers to a wire rack with a wide spatula.

Bake the remaining batter, using the same pans; they usually don't need to be rebuttered. Cool the crackers on a wire rack. Store in an airtight container, handling the delicate crackers gently.

The atmosphere in the kitchen at Joe's can often be hectic—feeding the crowds that flock to the restaurant is heavy-duty work.

THE COOKS

Unlike at most restaurants today, orders at Joe's aren't put in on "dupes"—the cooks aren't given written order slips. The waiters come through the kitchen and call out their orders, and the cooks put it all out by memory, without missing a beat. When you serve 1,800 dinners a night, that's no small feat.

Coconut Cream Pie

Use the Butter Pastry recipe below or your own favorite pie-crust recipe.

MAKES ONE 9-INCH PIE

Dough for 1 9-inch pastry
shell (recipe follows)
$2^{1}/_{3}$ cups grated coconut,
preferably fresh
$2^{1}/_{3}$ cups milk
$^{1}/_{4}$ cup light corn syrup
$^{1}/_{4}$ cup cornstarch
$^{1}/_{2}$ cup sugar

$^{1}/_{4}$ teaspoon salt
3 egg yolks
2 teaspoons pure vanilla
extract
$^{3}/_{4}$ cup heavy or whipping cream,
well chilled
2 tablespoons confectioners'
sugar

On a lightly floured board, roll pastry dough out to about $^{1}/_{8}$-inch thick; gently fit it into a buttered 9-inch pie pan. Trim off excess dough, leaving a slight overhang; fold the edge of the dough under along the rim of the pie plate, forming a high fluted border. Chill the pastry while you preheat the oven to 375°F, with a rack in the lower third of the oven.

Line the pastry dough with a lightly buttered sheet of foil, buttered side down. Bake the pastry for about 10 to 12 minutes, or until the sides have set. Gently remove the foil and continue to bake, pricking any air bubbles gently with a fork, until the crust is pale golden and just baked through, about 8 minutes longer (timing can vary; do not overbake). Cool the crust on a wire rack.

With the oven still at 375°F, place $1^{1}/_{2}$ cups of the coconut in a jelly roll pan and bake, stirring once or twice, until medium golden brown, about 9 minutes (watch carefully to prevent burning). Set aside on a wire rack to cool.

Scald 2 cups of the milk with the corn syrup in a heavy nonaluminum saucepan. In a mixing bowl, whisk the cornstarch with the sugar. Add the salt, yolks, and remaining $^{1}/_{3}$ cup of milk, whisking until well blended. Gradually pour the hot milk mixture into the bowl; then return the mixture to the saucepan over medium-low heat.

Whisk the mixture constantly until thickened; boil gently for 2 minutes. Remove from heat and stir in the remaining 1 cup of untoasted coconut and $1^{1}/_{2}$ teaspoons vanilla. Cool for 5 or 10 minutes, whisking now and then. Pour the mixture into the baked pie shell. Cool, then refrigerate.

Just before serving the pie, whip the cream until thickened; then add the confectioners' sugar and the remaining ½ teaspoon vanilla and whip until nearly stiff. Top the pie with the whipped cream, mounding it smoothly; then scatter the toasted coconut over the surface. Chill until ready to serve.

BUTTER PASTRY

1 ¼ cups all-purpose flour
¼ teaspoon salt
½ cup cold unsalted butter,
  cut into pieces

5 tablespoons ice water, or
  as needed

In a food processor or medium bowl, mix the flour and salt. Add the butter and mix together until crumbly. Add enough cold water for the dough to come together. Gather it into a ball; then wrap in plastic wrap and chill for at least ½ hour before using.

JOE'S COFFEE

David Young, who has been a waiter at Joe's on and off for fifteen years, has his own coffee importing business. He prepared a custom blend for Joe's coffee, both regular and decaf. "The blend has some Guatemalan beans," he explains, "some Costa Rican, a little Colombian and Kenyan. This gives it a balance, and it's roasted to a dark richness. We grind the beans fresh here, just before they're brewed, to give the freshest possible taste.

"I felt keenly aware that coffee is often one of the least-paid-attention-to aspects of restaurant menus. And it's one of the last memories that you carry with you as you leave. And it's such a shame, when it is really not a difficult thing to do. But it does need attention.

"A lot of times, coffee is relegated to the least skilled person on the staff. Here at Joe's, I'm happy to say that we have one person who's assigned to keep his eye on the coffee, to make sure that it is prepared properly, so you get consistency. So we pay attention. These kinds of things make a difference. I feel privileged that Jo Ann let me customize the roast for Joe's."

Key Lime Cake

A moist, golden cake with a tender crumb, tangy with lime, that keeps well. Joe's Key Lime Cake is adapted from a recipe in Linda Gassenheimer's *Keys Cuisine.* This recipe can be doubled and baked in a 12-inch Bundt pan.

MAKES ONE 8-INCH BUNDT CAKE, ABOUT 8 SERVINGS

1/2 cup unsalted butter, softened
1 cup sugar
Grated zest of 1 lime
2 eggs
1 3/4 cups all-purpose flour
1 teaspoon baking powder
1 teaspoon baking soda
1/2 teaspoon salt

2/3 cup plain low-fat yogurt
1 tablespoon lime juice

Syrup
1/3 cup freshly squeezed lime juice, preferably Key lime juice (2 to 3 limes)
2/3 cup confectioners' sugar, sifted

Preheat the oven to 350°F. Generously butter a 6-cup Bundt pan (about 8 inches), or use an 8-inch-square, 2-inch-deep cake pan; set aside.

In an electric mixer, beat the butter until smooth. Gradually add the sugar and lime zest, beating until light and fluffy. Add the eggs, one at a time, and continue to beat.

Meanwhile, sift the dry ingredients together onto a sheet of wax paper. Lower the mixer speed and add the flour alternately with the yogurt to the egg mixture, beginning and ending with the flour. Add the 1 tablespoon lime juice, mixing the batter just until blended, no longer.

Scrape the batter into the pan; smooth the top, and place on the center oven rack. Bake about 40 minutes, or until the cake is golden, a toothpick inserted in the center comes out clean, and the cake starts to pull away from the sides of the pan. (If the cake begins to brown before it has baked through, lay a sheet of foil loosely over the top.) Remove the pan from the oven and let stand on a wire rack for 10 minutes.

Meanwhile, make the syrup: Stir together the lime juice and confectioners' sugar until smooth.

Run a knife blade around the edges of the cake and invert it onto the rack, set over a large plate lined with wax paper. While the cake is still warm, slow-

spoon or brush the syrup over the top and sides of the cake so that all of the liquid is absorbed. Pour any drippings from the wax paper over the cake as well. If you like, just before serving, sprinkle with additional confectioners' sugar.

Bobby Moorehead, Lloyd Godwin, and Calvin Keel.

Matthew Johnson and Anthony Arneson at the maître d's desk.

*T*he employees at Joe's know, first of all, that all the policies, procedures, rules, and guidelines are all fair.

There are also so many benefits and perks here at Joe's, compared to other restaurants. There's a profit-sharing plan, three bonuses a year for all the employees; the restaurant has, in times of emergency, extended a hand to employees. And all the employees have a kind of a common bond of success here, where everybody works together. I think it's the family touch that's made Joe's as successful as it is.

—Anthony Arneson, day maître d'

EAT AT JOE'S

Celebrities Who Have Enjoyed Joe's Stone Crabs

1920s–1940s

Damon Runyon
Sophie Tucker
Gene Tierney
Jimmy Dorsey
Tommy Dorsey
Eddie Rickenbacker
Amelia Earhart
Franklin D. Roosevelt
Duke and Duchess
  of Windsor
J. Edgar Hoover
Calvin Coolidge
Warren G. Harding
Richard Barthelmess
André Kostelanetz
Al Capone
Walter Winchell
Meyer Lansky
Al Jolson
Charles Lindbergh
Guy Lombardo
Gloria Swanson
Joseph P. Kennedy
Anna May Wong
Clark Gable
Gene Tunney
Heywood Hale Broun
Jack Dempsey
Jimmy Walker
William Powell
Thomas Dewey

1950s–1960s

William Paley
Jock Whitney
George Bourke
Rita Hayworth
Orson Welles
Bing Crosby
Ralph J. Bunche
Dorothy Lamour
Jackie Gleason
Jack Paar
Arthur Godfrey
Milton Berle
Nicky Hilton
Mike Todd
Elizabeth Taylor
Eddie Fisher
Debbie Reynolds
James Michener
Burt Lancaster
John F. Kennedy

1970s–1990s

Joel Grey
Ann-Margret
Jimmy Buffet
Don Johnson
Melanie Griffith
Billy Joel
Christie Brinkley
Bob Griese
Larry Csonka
Dan Marino

Julio Iglesias
Barbra Streisand
Candice Bergen
Louis Malle
Tom Brokaw
Ed Bradley
Walter Cronkite
Al Martino
George and
  Barbara Bush
Dan Quayle
Jack Kemp
Itzhak Perlman
Mikhail Baryshnikov
Sting
Darryl Hall
John Oates
Walter Payton
Princess Caroline
Larry King
Bill Murray
Dennis Miller
Gary Player
Gene Barry
Donald Sutherland
Robert Duvall
Kevin Costner
Madonna
Bill Clinton
Luciano Pavarotti
Gloria and Emilio
  Estefan

The wait, the shared anticipation, is part of the taste of the food, standing there staring into whole rooms full of people in bibs hunched over plates of hash browns and cracked claws. Dipping. Munching. Sucking. The essence, the heart of Miami all here, the whole life experience, birth to death, bib to bib, with waiting in between.

—*"Mr. Peeper's Nights: Anxiety in the Sun,"*
New York *magazine, January 18, 1993*

EAT AT JOE'S

ABOUT THOSE WAITS

Joe's Stone Crabs takes no reservations. By five o'clock every afternoon, there are people lined up outside, waiting for the restaurant to open for dinner. The infamous waits can be two hours or even longer. Roy Garret, the maître d', is jokingly introduced at civic functions as "the second most powerful man in Miami, after the mayor."

"I came here temporarily twenty-two years ago," Roy says. "I'm still here. There were already long waits then. Every place I go, anywhere in the world, I see people I know from Joe's."

Allan Myerson tells a story: "Jesse walked into my office one morning after we closed for the season. He said, 'Allan, would you believe last night there was a bird flying around the dining room.' I said, 'You're kidding! How did it get in?' He said, 'He duped Roy a sawbuck.' "

What can you do to minimize the wait? Roy: "Well, it's very simple. Everybody in the world wants to eat between seven and nine. The smartest thing to do is to come before seven or after nine."

In a story called "Getting Stoned" ("The Shocking Truth about Getting a Table at Joe's") in *Tropic*, the *Miami Herald*'s Sunday magazine, humorist Dave Barry recounts trying several methods to see if he could get a table without a long wait. He calls the restaurant

On the cover of the issue of the *Miami Herald Tropic* that lampooned the long waits at Joe's.

Joe's Extremely Famous Stone Crab Restaurant in South Miami Beach. A Landmark. A Legend. . . . THE place to see and be seen. Everybody goes there. In fact, the big mystery surrounding the South Florida visit of Pope John Paul II was: How come he never went to Joe's? He'd have got a table very quickly. Minutes after he walked in, the loudspeaker would have said: "Mr. II, party of 173, your table is ready."

Barry designated one couple as "the control couple," ready to wait however long it took. A second couple (including himself in disguise) would tell "The Man" at the front desk, "I'll take care of you on the way out." The third would "try to give The Man a $20 bill right up front, displaying no subtlety whatsoever.

"Conclusions: Draw your own. . . . It would probably not be a real smart move to mention my name."

Bibliography

Bishop, Ann M. Transcript of taped interviews with Jesse Weiss. 1982.

Davidson, Alan. *Seafood*. New York: Simon & Schuster, 1989.

Fleming, Ian. *Goldfinger*. New York: Macmillan, 1959.

Gassenheimer, Linda. *Keys Cuisine*. New York: Atlantic Monthly Press, 1991.

Henry, Bruce. "The Gentry Eats Crabs." *Esquire*, February 1939.

Hiaasen, Carl. *Tourist Season*. New York: G. P. Putnam's Sons, 1986.

King, Larry. *Tell It to the King*. New York: G. P. Putnam's Sons, 1988.

Leonard, Elmore. *La Brava*. New York: Arbor House, 1983.

Loomis, Susan Herrmann. *The Great American Seafood Cookbook*. New York: Workman, 1988.

Marcus, Stanley. *Quest for the Best*. New York: Viking, 1979.

Parks, Arva Moore. *Miami—Marching with the Drums*. Miami: Barnett Bank, 1990.

Paar, Jack. *P.S. Jack Paar*. New York: Doubleday, 1982.

Redford, Polly. *Billion-Dollar Sandbar—A Biography of Miami Beach*. New York: E. P. Dutton, 1970.

Sewell, John. *Miami Memoirs (A New Pictorial Edition by Arva Moore Parks)*. Miami: Arva Moore Parks (with Lion & Thorne Ltd., Tulsa, Oklahoma), 1987.

Smiley, Nixon. *Yesterday's Miami*. Miami: E. A. Seemann, 1973.

Stern, Ellen. "Romancing the Stone Crab." *GQ*, February 1987.

Index